HOW TO INDIVIDUALIZE KINDERGARTEN TEACHING

New Approaches Using the Key Sensory Modes

HOW TO INDIVIDUALIZE KINDERGARTEN TEACHING

New Approaches
Using the
Key Sensory Modes

BERNICE C. HOLLAND

99848

Parker Publishing Company, Inc.
West Nyack, New York

Library of Congress Cataloging in Publication Data

Holland, Bernice C.
  How to individualize kindergarten teaching.

  Bibliography: p.
  1. Kindergarten--Methods and manuals. 2. Individualized instruction. I. Title.
LB1169.H54   372.1'3'94   74-647

THE SCOPE AND VALUE
OF THIS BOOK

This book will enable teachers in early education to use individualized activities and exercises that are related to the key sensory modes of learning, and to provide ways to insure individualized instruction. Ignoring the sensory modes of perception can cause some children to be unable to participate in an adequate way. Children have such individual needs in so many areas that a teacher must have many approaches and techniques to satisfy their needs. Teachers have had to research the auditory, visual, or motor perceptual training techniques from a variety of sources. Much valuable time can be saved by using the resource material included in this book.

Children come to school with such widespread abilities, skills, and backgrounds that there is a great need for approaches that are based on sensory modes and individualized instruction. Their individual needs may be motor, auditory, or visual, with related memory and reasoning abilities. They do not all respond in the same way to one set of directions. They are well aware, in their own way, of their differences in ability, making it essential for each one to have pride in what he is able to do. For each feeling of pride in accomplishment, an increased effort to succeed will follow. For some who try to perform at all times with equal degrees of success with the full group, the label of "slow learner" is

7

applied. Labeling can be a dangerous and damaging process. There must be methods to provide individualized instruction whether it is on a one-to-one basis or in a group situation.

If a child's motor, auditory, and visual needs are neglected, leaving him uncoordinated and not able to react intelligently, his chances for learning are minimal. Too much delay in these areas may create emotional involvements difficult to overcome. By using the methods that are suggested here it has been possible to have each child in every class progress to a higher level of learning. The basic sensory modes of learning are approached here in relation to appropriate activities and exercises. There are ways suggested to use the services of older students and parents in order to give the children the necessary individual time.

In addition to the children with learning difficulties, there are those with social or behavioral problems that may disrupt the classroom situation. Methods that have proved repeatedly to help these children are given. They have been successful in crowded classes, and even with children previously rejected in other places as "not ready to fit into a group situation." Many have learned to become important, responsible members of a group.

The ages five to seven are crucial years. They are known by psychologists as the habit-forming years because more lasting habits are formed during this period than at any other time. This makes it vital for the teacher to be as fully prepared as possible. This book points up the need to know by what sensory mode a child may learn best so that he may experience success and gain confidence, and then to afford opportunities for individualized instruction to care for these differences. It indicates the necessity for a happy, relaxed, learning atmosphere to have the school become a desirable place to be.

The goal in kindergarten is the same as that for any grade level of instruction. It is to know each child's level and abilities and take him from there at the rate he can most comfortably perform. It is to build into the child a feeling of worth and importance. No matter how small his contribution may be, he can develop to his maximum ability only when he realizes that he and his thinking are important. This is the type of positive reinforcement that is stressed in this book.

The practical ideas presented here are not only for students who have learning difficulties—they can also enable the accelerated students to reach their potential. The children of this age have such a desire to learn, they must be kept reaching while experiencing success.

Bernice C. Holland

ACKNOWLEDGMENTS

I express my gratitude to the many friends who encouraged me to write this book. I wish to thank the willing victims who critiqued some of the chapters—Leonard Davis, Pat Forde, Nancy McVicker, Margaret Taylor—because I consider them to be experts in their fields of learning. I especially wish to thank Joe Del Quadri, School Psychologist, Department of Special Education at the University of Oregon, not only for his generous giving of time to discuss and critique chapters, but for the inspiration his personal dedication creates in others to further the education of children.

CONTENTS

10. Creating in Art 157

11. Experiments in Science 183

Index 201

ANALYZING KEY FACTORS THAT SIMPLIFY INDIVIDUALIZED INSTRUCTION

1

Any kindergarten class comes with a variety of interests, behavioral patterns, and abilities. Some will be eager, outgoing children; some will be shy loners. There will be those worrying about the sort of person you may be. Then, too, you may have the independent one used to doing everything when he wants to and in the way he wants. A tearful, protesting child may also be part of your classroom. With such an assortment of personalities, it is essential to be as well prepared as possible and to have conditions ready that will afford the happy introduction to school that is so vital to children.

The teacher must get to know something about the general background of the children. She must not only devise ways to get to know each individual child, but must plan an introduction that will enable the children to feel that she is a friend. Carefully prepared plans for the first day are crucial. The teacher must establish the behavioral and work patterns for optimum classroom conditions from the start. To obtain the best possible rapport, there should be means to foster the interest of parents in the work of their children. With the many divergent needs of any beginning group of children, there should be arrangements made to provide individualized instruction.

This book contains a large number of activities that will aid in the development of the different areas of learning. All children will not be able to perform all tasks with equal degrees of success. The activities should be selected for the children according to their levels of ability. They may not all be doing the same task, or at the same level, at the same time. When you observe a child having difficulties with any of the activities, that is the signal for you to provide individual help.

At various times the children should be allowed to select the activities they wish to perform. The period I call the Activity (or Work) Period is especially suited for this. Other periods during the day can also be used when children make their choices of specific tasks. During the "Readiness" period they can at times choose from a variety of activities previously done. They may have different science materials to choose for experiments, or there may be number games or visual activities to select.

While the children are working individually. you can work with those who need assistance—or have aides work with them in their areas of need.

In the activities that follow, every time you see a child who is unable to function as well as the others, work with him, or have him join a group, or have an aide work with him. Another child may also be able to help.

PRODUCTIVE TECHNIQUES FOR GETTING TO KNOW EACH STUDENT

Knowing your school neighborhood (walk through it or drive around) and knowing the general community background can furnish clues to the types of children you can expect to have in your class. You may need to be prepared for a different level of approach if you know there will be language problems, or if you will be meeting children with rich backgrounds of experience, or those with a minimal level of experience.

A teacher who has taught in the same school for a number of years has somewhat of an advantage. She not only knows the general type of children to expect, but entering children often have a sense of being acquainted, or an idea of what they may expect.

Getting Acquainted Before the New Term

Some teachers try to become acquainted with many of the next group by planning a springtime classroom visit for them. This should not be a time to show all the work the present class can do as this could frighten some future pupils by having them think they would be expected to perform that way when they first started school. Rather, it should be a time that has been planned, with the assistance of the class, to share some simple activities with the visitors. The kindergarten children share the responsibility for trying to have all the guests involved in something. They can share some uncomplicated games, puzzles, blocks, drawing, etc., while the teacher circulates and visits with the newcomers. The class might entertain them with some songs and serve cookies. The teacher can read a story for all to enjoy before the visitors leave. A 45-minute to one-hour time period should be sufficient to give the children a feeling of being acquainted while not tiring anyone. It is less disrupting to have a get-acquainted meeting in one planned session than to permit children to be brought to spend a day at just any time. The kindergarten has a program of work to accomplish and should be recognized with the same respect and dignity other grades enjoy.

A teacher new to the community might have a get-acquainted meeting planned through the principal and P.T.A. Some have had the mothers cooperate by planning a cookie and ice cream picnic at a local park. Others prefer to meet at the school. The gathering is to give the children a feeling of knowing the teacher as a friend, or at least, to avoid the total-stranger feeling. Some teachers establish a feeling of friendship with a new group by mailing little notes of welcome shortly before school is to start. A note in the mail is a big event for a five-year-old. Several children have clutched the notes in their hands on the first day of school.

Another getting-acquainted method is to have a play-day shortly before the closing of the school year and to invite future students to come. This can be held on the playground. Older children can help organize group games to prevent one person having too many children to control at one time. Aides can also assist the shy ones by getting them involved in games and activities. This gives the teacher free time to observe or talk with new students. Then all could go to the kindergarten room for a quiet story or treat before leaving.

EASY WAYS TO PREPARE FOR THE
CRUCIAL FIRST DAY AND
INDIVIDUAL DIFFERENCES

Since the first day of school is of such vital importance to the child and any new learning situation should have optimum conditions to insure success, great care should be given in planning this time. Kindergarten children are facing their introduction to formal education. Many behavioral patterns necessary in a group situation are still to be learned. When a large group of inexperienced young children is suddenly confined and expected to cooperate in some manner, the teacher finds herself in the position of being forced to immediately establish some "do" and "don't" rules, and to try to mold the children into a performing group. Although children must learn acceptable patterns of behavior, they must also retain their individuality and the sense of individual importance and dignity.

Sizes of Groups for Optimum Initial Conditions

Desirable behavioral patterns are best established in a natural and positive way if the first class meetings take place in small, divided groups for periods of time. The children are more relaxed and the teacher gets to know individuals, all of which leads to a much smoother beginning. Learning is actually accelerated with a small, relaxed, happy group. With a more gradual introduction, by the end of two weeks, the class can become adjusted to routines and the group situation. This greatly lessens the possibility of having some frightened children who take a month to calm down. This often happens when many children are thrust in at once to stay for a full session. Some schools use the first week, or even two, for this gradual introduction.

When so much time cannot be allowed to ease the children into the new situation, a method that can at least be a big help is to use the first two days for this introduction. Both morning and afternoon sessions are divided in half, resulting in four groups meeting on the first day. This is explained to the parents when they register the child. Letters are sent out before school begins to inform the parents of the time they are to bring their children in on the first day. The first group meets for one hour. The parent is asked to plan to stay in the room for that hour. There is a 30-minute break to prepare for the second group's hour. After the noon intermission, the same schedule is repeated for the afternoon groups. A parent (or responsible adult) is to be with each child. This assures the child's feeling of security, and also his getting home safely. It also affords the teacher an opportunity to talk to the parents a bit, and a chance for parents to ask questions.

Most parents appreciate this getting-acquainted time. They often have questions you may not expect, and satisfying their needs can result in having a better relationship with the children. For bus children, the parents may ride the bus, or meet it, to make certain the children know where to get off. Each bus child should have a name and address tag on his coat until the driver gets to know him. The walking children are instructed about patrols and crossings and are then asked to show their parents they know the route they are to travel.

On the second day have the full morning group come for the first hour while the mothers meet in some other room with the principal and some P.T.A. members for a coffee visit. Use the same routine for the afternoon group. The first day the children are in a small group with mother close by in the room. The second day they experience the large group for a short time, knowing mother is in the building. This helps the worried child a great deal and usually eliminates tears.

Obviously, if the four sessions a day could be continued for a week, much progress could be made in getting to know each child. There could be a better understanding of individual needs. The shy child would have a better chance for attention instead of being "lost" in the crowd before he could feel secure. The teacher can then tend to each child's needs if the class size is kept between 20 and 25.

Getting to know the name of each child establishes a friendly feeling and makes the child feel important. The sooner you can know their names the better. One suggestion is to make headbands with the names on them. On the second day have the class gather after hanging up their wraps. As you call their names, each child can come to you for you to measure and staple the band. Then, each time you look at the child, you see his name. The next day you can use the headbands for roll call and pass them out as you read the names.

Room Preparation

Getting ready for that crucial first day requires the teacher to have her room prepared in advance. It should be as attractive as possible. Bright, gay pictures should be mounted. There can be bulletin boards such as "Fun in Kindergarten" with labeled sections; "Blocks," with cutouts of blocks; "Music," having a staff and notes; "Numbers," using a few numerals; "Colors," putting up colored shapes; "Painting," with a picture. Another could be "Welcome to School" having large pictures of Mary and her lamb with a stylized school house. "Stories We Like" could be the title for a bulletin board. Mount pictures of favorite nursery rhymes or old, well-known stories.

If birthdays are to be recognized, a list of September birthday names can be attractively prepared. This list is explained to the group on the first day when they are gathered together.

Traffic safety is a "Must" so it is appropriate to have a traffic sign on display to discuss before going home.

For the first day, do not put too many materials out in the classroom. There should be enough to create interest while at the same time avoiding confusion. Limiting what is available for use also promotes the orderliness the children should learn from the start. It leaves materials to be added gradually for interest and affords the opportunity to introduce new materials by showing their proper use. Arranged playhouse equipment is inviting. Two or three small toys will attract some children. Have a few interesting things on a science table—possibly some shells, a bird nest, some interesting rocks, or driftwood. Put out some easy puzzles, picture books, pegs and boards, beads and strings, paper, crayons, clay with clay boards. You may have some uncomplicated type of construction toy or a small flannel board with cut-outs. These things are easily controlled and can be satisfactorily used in a short period of time.

Establishing Relationships and Behavioral Attitudes

On the first day, as the small group comes, greet each child directly to make him feel noticed and welcome. Some little personal comment might help. Ask, then, for any nicknames, as some have only learned to respond to nicknames. Show the children where to put their coats. Suggest to each one that he take his mother around the room to show her what he will have to use. Let him know that anything available may be used if he chooses. This indicates to the child it is his room and mother is his guest. When they are told, "This is your room to share; any of the things are for you to use; take your mother around the room so she can see some of the fun things you may be doing; let her know what you choose,'' the child is given the lead and the importance. Naturally, some will expect mother to do the leading, but most mothers get the message. When the child decides on something he wants to use, he may do so. Mother may sit by him, or in some other place, according to the child's decision. This is a time to note the ones leaving and the ones clinging to mother.

After the children are settled at something—some in groups and some close to mother—walk around to chat with different ones. You are bound to note a generally quiet tone due to the small group and the new situation. This is a good time to establish the desirable pattern of voice level. Praise them for the "kindergarten way" they are talking. This begins your positive reinforcement. You may act surprised that they already know so much about the polite way to act in a group. This will amaze some who have never before heard praise for their actions with others. For them it can be most effective. Praise goes a long way. You may even ask if they have ever been in school before, because they are doing so nicely. Their ego is lifted and even the less cooperative ones usually try to show what they can do. You must act the part. Sound sincere and surprised when it is called for. This is a good opportunity for some mothers to notice, for the first time, their children's behavior in a new group. You will note the very shy or very noisy ones and be prepared to care for their individual needs.

When the group is busily occupied, this is a good time to tell them that since they are so quiet you can get to visit with their mothers. You may have special things to explain—routines, or things the children should bring. You may want to tell parents about a special way you celebrate birthdays (some do not approve of this) or to explain plans you may have for mother-helpers and how mothers may select a helping time. There should be a time to let the mothers ask questions. Children think they know what is theirs, but coats, sneakers, and boots do look so much alike, so request to have them labeled.

After a short activity time, during part of which you talked with the mothers, tap a bell or use some signal that is to be used *only* when the group is to stop what they are doing and come quickly to you. Of course, the first time you do this, some children will just look your way. Then be surprised for those who "already know the important bell and stopped to look." "In fact, you did so well, I am going to wait a little and try it again to see if you all can stop when I tap the signal.'' A few seconds later, at another tap, give more praise for attention and then explain that the bell means you have something important to say and would like to have them leave what they are doing and come to you. ''Do you suppose you can do that on *just your first day here?* I won't tell you when, but I'll try it.'' About five seconds later, tap the bell. As some come, praise them. Some may hang back, but finally come. ''That was so good, I want to try again. Mothers, see how well your children are learning. I won't tell when I'll tap again.'' Have the children go back to what they were doing, then try again. Give more praise; have mothers praise the children too. If there is a shy one who didn't make it, you can say you enjoyed what the children did so much you want to try it *one* more time before you tell them the important thing you had to say. Then stroll over by the shy one and tap the bell. ''What do you know! We all are here!'' The shy one usually looks surprised at how he made it, but he gets in on the praise and that seems to end his holding back for the bell. Then tell them what the important thing was. ''It is time to put away the things you used just the way you found them. Then come back to me because we have more important things to hear.''

When everything is put away, you can show the children around the room and explain classroom procedures, such as a safe way to carry chairs when it is necessary. Then have them come in a group, either with chairs or on a rug. The first day is the time to let the children know the way you want them to sit. It is much easier to learn it one way than to try to break habits later and relearn. You reinforce their efforts by commenting on how much they are learning.

When all are in a group you can give a feeling of learning something special by teaching a short finger game. An easy one that uses circles and counting is:

''Here's a ball,'' (make a circle with thumb and forefinger).

''And here's a ball,'' (then a larger circle with both hands).

''And a great big ball I see,'' (large circle with both arms).

''Shall we count them? Are you ready?''

''One—two—three,'' (repeat actions).

As time permits, discuss traffic safety and identify the traffic colors. Have some find the colors in the room or on the other children. If you have a birthday chart, explain it. There may be time for a short phonograph record. Read a short story, being sure it is on the early level.

Then explain the best way for getting coats and getting ready to go home. Teach them to avoid jumping up and running around in confusion.

When they are ready to leave tell the group, "Tomorrow we will have some different things to learn and you will meet more friends." Then remind them of the important things they have learned on their first day: quiet voices, coming at the tap of a bell, cleaning up and putting away what they have used, and the finger game. Make it sound important.

These shortened sessions, with less things to use and do, afford a positive approach. If the children are relaxed and the teacher can use this time to get to know individual children and to establish basic orders and routines of behavior in a positive way, the learning process can be greatly accelerated.

Use the same activity materials during the first week. Each day have different ways to use the traffic colors and counting. Use new finger games and stories. Use the calendar. Establish an order of activity progression.

DEVELOPING EFFECTIVE BEHAVIORAL
AND WORK PATTERNS

As will be developed in Chapter 2, the teacher is a model for behavior. If she is relaxed, happy, and talks softly, she is more apt to draw similar responses.

While you have your small groups, comment on the quiet voices you hear. This is far better than drawing attention to any loud voices. Praise those who walk to someone to talk instead of calling out. Tell the group about the polite and orderly behaviors you notice. Notice those who wait politely for turns and give praise. Draw attention to all the satisfactory patterns of action. If a noisy child is quiet for a time, let him know you liked it when he was quiet. He will enjoy the praise. The first few days children can be doing some of their most important learning if they establish good behavioral patterns. Without these, there will be little academic learning taking place later.

The signal for getting the group to you should be repeated, after a reminder, for two or three days to reinforce it. Then, during the year, when work time is over and you want the group to gather, a little tap gets them together quickly for any discussion of work. Be sure you show pleasure for their coming quickly while the children are learning to respond. This establishes a habit that is a great boon throughout the year. The special signal must be used *only* when you want them to come to you and must not be overdone. Once, maybe twice a day is enough. Do not use it just to get attention. Teach a different signal, such as a piano chord, that may be used occasionally for attention.

Establishing the Uses of Materials

When you feel that the group is organized and works reasonably well together, add the blocks, after explaining the way they are to be handled. You could demonstrate different ways to put blocks down and let the children tell you what is best. Put out a few paint colors—the colors you are trying to teach. Show the group the way the paints should be handled and how you expect cleaning up to be done. Each time you add more materials to use, give some ideas for their use and care. Be sure you follow up so the children do not ignore regulations.

Add a game or a new material one at a time so that all will know what is available and will have time to try it. Too much at once scatters their interests and some may never get to see and use all the materials provided.

There are various ways to get the children to use all activity areas. One is to have a chart: Table 1—Painting; Table 2—Floor Toys; Table 3—Table Games, etc., according to the table situation. Have one table for Free Choice. Table choices rotate every day. Children soon get to anticipate what they will be doing the next day.

Another method is to limit the number of children for each activity. Have them put their name cards in a slot by the pictured activity if a place there is left. Keep a record so you know what each one has been doing. A different method is to make a chart for each child. These can be duplicated on 9x12 paper. The charts are passed out before work is chosen and have as many squares as there are activities: a little sketch to represent the work area is at the top of each square; some blocks for Block Building; scissors and paste for Cutting and Pasting; a house for Playhouse; a table for Table Games; etc. The children decide on the work they want to do that day and check the box. They must watch to see that they are not getting all their marks in just a few areas. You should go around while the charts are out to talk things over with the children.

With any method decided upon, the children should understand that they should finish any work started if it isn't finished at the end of one session and is something that can be saved for another day.

Early in the year, before children are planning their own activities for the next day, it is important to have some new activities for them to anticipate. You do not have to tell them what it is to be, just say, "There will be something new on the science table," or, "We will learn a new game." Keep anticipation alive.

The security of a planned routine is important to establish a better attitude towards work and also to set behavioral patterns as routines are established. A general daily routine should begin immediately. Naturally, there are times when the pattern will be broken or changed; however, if it is generally followed, things tend to go more smoothly.

Planning a Daily Schedule

A daily schedule is a personal thing; what works well for one may not suit another. You may want to hold the activity period early in the day, before fatigue sets in. This often turns what might have been a noisy time into a quiet time. Save the less tiresome activities for later, for the more tired the children are, the more restless and noisy they become. A relaxed child is able to sit and move quietly. Within the planned schedule, you can plan your individualized instruction.

A routine that has proved to be balanced as to quiet and active periods follows:

1. Opening—10 minutes
   Attendance; Calendar; Recognizing any birthday; Counting the group.
2. Show and Tell—15 minutes
   This can be a true learning situation. Children gain ability to speak before a group, express themselves clearly, think on their feet, plan their presentation, and respect turns if it is organized. Have a card for each child. Turn up the bottom card of the stack and ask that child if he wants a turn for the next day. If he does, the name goes in a slot on the Show and Tell chart. He is to plan at home something about which he can tell at least three things. He may just tell if he doesn't want to bring something. Four names are put up. A child may refuse a turn. At Show and Tell time sit in back of the group and have a child, as a helper, hold up

a card from the chart and then bring it to you. When a child has his turn, date the card on the back and use a code to recall whether he merely enumerated facts, became descriptive, or advanced to interpreting what he told in relation to other events. In this way you have a running record of the child's speaking and planning ability. The group is expected to be polite during turns because an impolite child misses his turn if his name comes up next. The speaker is to look around for attention before beginning. With polite attention it can be surprising how well the shy child responds and gains confidence before the group. With the teacher in back, it becomes the children's activity. They enjoy self-control and feel more mature.

3. Activity Time (or Chosen Work)—25 minutes
    Work by chart, free choice, or however you feel is best to have activities. The children make their own choices as to specific tasks.
4. Showing Work Done and Clean Up—10 minutes
5. Readiness—15-20 minutes
    Early in the year this can be matching colors, learning finger games, counting, numeral matching games, learning shapes, or using the sensory mode activities suggested. Individualized instruction can be going on by the use of aides.
6. Recess—Rest
    If you have less than a 2½ hour session, this can be omitted.
7. Songs—15 minutes
8. Rhythms—15 minutes
9. Stories—15 minutes
10. Getting Ready to Leave—5 minutes

The times indicated can easily be lengthened or shortened. There are occasions when the activity of a period is such that it has too much value and interest to be stopped at a fixed time. At other times, something unexpected can happen, bringing about an opportunity for a meaningful experience. The daily routine is not a rigid and unchangeable schedule; rather, it is a guide. Surprise changes in a schedule are fun, and having fun while learning is important. There is no harm in eliminating one period of activity on one day. It is better to omit an activity than to try to crowd it in for a brief, rushed time.

Give the children some specific time for pursuing their own interests (a la Open Classroom). This may be working with art materials, the science table, musical instruments, etc.

The fire drill should be explained and practiced during the first week to avoid panic later. To eliminate fear, explain that the fire drill is just to make sure that everyone will know the safe way to leave. They *walk* quickly and quietly out the nearest door to a designated place, away from the building. The teacher must be the last one out to be certain that no one has remained inside. After explaining the drill, lead the children through it. Then have them try it by taking the lead.

One very satisfactory way to establish the idea that each child is competing only with himself, and to avoid any unnecessary criticism of another's work, is to provide individual folders for saving samples of work. During the first or second week, have the children draw a house and a person for you to save. Let them know this work will be saved and that it will be returned at the end of the year. The pictures are made without help or directions. They indicate the child's ability at that time. Then, possibly two months later, pass out the folders and have each child look at the pictures he did before. Ask for another drawing of a house and a person. Number each page to be able to compare it with later work. Let them know it will be tried again later on. Each time the folders are given out, the earlier work is to be observed to see if what was done previously can be improved. The folders are also used to save samples of different types of work in order to have a fair cross-section of paper work, including art, to permit the children to use their own work for self comparison. The children are reminded to look only at their own work and not to worry about what their neighbor has done. This offers a good means for the teacher to observe individual progress and is something to use at a conference time.

HOW TO GET PARENTS ACTIVELY INVOLVED

Having parents help in the classroom offers many advantages. Some teachers may feel that having another person in the room would bother them and they would be more relaxed working alone. Some parents also have feelings of timidity toward a teacher. These are common barriers that should come down. When parents and teachers work together in a room, a feeling of friendship is a natural result. There are many ways a parent can be of real help and at the same time they are able to observe their children in the classroom situation. When parents are introduced as helpers and are active in the room the children do not regard them as visitors.

Getting the parents actively involved can be introduced in a letter before school begins in the fall. This can be included in the notice telling about the time schedule for the children. They will have some time to think it over and possibly get their thinking adjusted in favor of volunteering their help. The letter should give a general idea of the help wanted: passing out materials or helping to prepare them after being shown how; circulating during activity time; helping children as needed when they are trying to make something that the teacher has demonstrated; helping with games or exercises. Point out the advantages helping can offer, for example, being able to see, in a normal situation, their child's behavior and work. Children gain interest and pride when they know their parents are concerned and involved. These advantages for the parents serve in the same measure for the teacher.

On the first day of school have some sort of chart ready to show the parents where they may sign for regular turns. Younger children are not to accompany the parent on the helping day because that causes too much distraction. One or two parents at a session would be enough. Once or twice a month may be sufficient for a parent's turn. The friendly feelings established among parents, teacher, and child are of very positive value.

The parents are requested to spend no more time in the room with their own child than with other children. In fact, by being with other children most of the time, their own child is soon able to appear unaware of the parent's presence. The class becomes so adjusted to having adult helpers in the room that they are apt to ask any adult who might just happen to come into the room for any assistance that might be needed at the time.

WHY, WHEN, AND HOW TO USE AIDES

Individual attention is very necessary for a child in kindergarten. He not only has many tasks to perform and skills to develop that are new for him, but he has just come from the situation of home life where the attention he received was mostly in a one-to-one situation. The sudden change of being just one member in a large group can be traumatic for some children. It is generally easier for children to share "things" than to share themselves easily. They listen better and show better understanding and retention when they are approached personally. During the first year children are not only learning facts and ways to deal with them, but they are developing attitudes toward school and acquiring a self-rating of their own abilities. Being in a large class of children, some tend to get "lost." They do not assert themselves and are apt to miss much of what happens.

Older students as well as adults may be of help to children in the classroom. Some older students may have problems in the same areas of learning that the beginning learner has: hearing sounds, sequential memory, etc. Helping others has proved to be an extra bonus for them as they must prepare for the lesson and, thus, often acquire skills they had missed.

Aides can be of service during any part of the session. They may be in the room helping certain children while you are busy with others; they may be using material that is similar to the task being done by the group, but on a one-to-one basis; they may be working on a special need; they may also be of service during the time the children have free choice of activities to tend to general supplies, thus leaving you free to assist the children; or, during an exercise or game time, an aide can be directing the group while another is assisting individuals needing perceptual-motor help.

To use the services of aides to the best advantage, plans must be made carefully. The aides must have thorough instruction in regard to the material to be presented, the method of presentation, and how to record results that provide a means for evaluation.

If your school is fortunate in having a counselor, she can be of great service training or recruiting volunteers and helping with record keeping. The counselor can also test to identify specific needs.

SUMMARY

● The teacher must be as well informed as possible about a new group and have optimum conditions for the introduction to school.

● She must immediately establish her positive methods of control and relationships.

● There must be a feeling of rapport with the parents and an effort to get them involved with the work at school.

● The teacher must have plans made to provide individual instruction as it is needed.

ESTABLISHING
AN INDIVIDUALIZED
LEARNING ATMOSPHERE

2

No matter what equipment you may have, how many interesting ideas you may present, or how attractive your classroom may be, without a learning atmosphere very little desirable learning will take place. In fact, undesirable habits can be formed, such as ignoring directions, failing to pay attention, or disregarding the rights of others.

The teacher must realize that she is a model for the behavioral patterns she hopes to instill in the class. She must be sure of the goals she hopes to achieve and consistent in her manner from the first day on to be able to reach these goals. Her most effective device will be her consistently confident, positive approach. It is important for a teacher to be prepared with measures that can curb individual behavioral problems. She should be able to recognize other learning hindrances that are not caused by problems of behavior, ability, or attitude.

DEVELOPING DESIRED ATTITUDES
EARLY IN THE YEAR

The general behavioral patterns should be started on the first day of school. Children are happier and feel more secure when they realize that there is a friendly and helpful person in control. While the teacher shows a happy, welcoming manner, she does so in a natural way to avoid overstimulation and also to avoid frightening off very shy children. The younger or less secure the child is the more he wants time to study an adult quietly to form his own feelings of trust. The child must be recognized as an individual and permitted to show his confidence when he is ready.

On the first day of school, some of the desired patterns of behavior should receive comments when they are observed—"What nice quiet voices you are using," "You really know how to wait politely for a turn," "I read a story only when everyone is listening quietly, and I can tell you enjoy stories." It is neither necessary nor helpful to sit a class down and list a set of rules they will be learning. But when a basic behavior pattern is established as the satisfactory way to act you must adhere to it. From the first day there must be a well-planned program that fosters in the children the realization of the learning taking place. It can be helpful and encouraging, during the first week, to tell the children just before they leave of the many important things that were done at school that day. Whether it is about learning some subject matter, coming when the bell was tapped, or the way they handled themselves in the room, children need assurance that they are making progress. Young people often do not recognize the subtle learning that takes place in the classroom.

Mutual respect for opinions and efforts should be evident, not only between teacher and children, but also within the group of children. A desired type of order shows courtesy as a matter of routine. The attitudes of attention, effort, and cooperation should be evident.

For a teacher to have a good relationship with her pupils, she must establish rapport with the parents. It is important for a teacher to know how to meet and confer with parents. She should not assume an attitude of knowing all the answers to all of the problems, but while offering possible suggestions, she should accept some as well. By being a listener, the causes of many problems may be revealed if the parents can feel secure that their confidences will not be violated.

WAYS TO PROMOTE DESIRED BEHAVIOR
WITH THE TEACHER AS A MODEL

Children tend to pattern their actions after behavioral practices that attract attention or get recognition. This often comes from observing the actions and reactions caused by others in the group. But the teacher, too, is a model for behavioral patterns. She must be consistent and sincere. When she shows sincere interest and a readiness to help, without undue concern for mistakes, she can create that attitude in the group. When she explains, "We all make mistakes, I do, too; but we are here to help each other," the group will reflect her happiness for good responses and will not laugh or criticize when errors are made. She does not get upset and draw undue attention to errors of work or behavior. The teacher shows her confidence in the children by her calm and positive manner.

Children tend to produce that behavior which they feel is expected or, at least, tolerated. If the teacher expects a normally quiet room she uses a soft voice, and she walks to people during an activity period to talk to them rather than calling across the room. She will not respond when someone calls to her, but will indicate that he should come up to speak to her. If she wants the children to be patient and show friendly responses, she must be the first one to consistently use these manners.

A Case in Point

Dave, behaving in extremely negative ways from the day he entered, produced mediocre work. He indicated a mistrust of adults by the way he cringed and ducked when he was approached. He was quietly and firmly stopped for any extreme behavior, but he also got a smile and praise for any good actions, no matter how ordinary they were. The friendly adult-to-child relationship obviously puzzled him. He would stare at children getting a pat or a hug, but would pull away when he was approached. At the end of the third month of school, he stayed back and watched the others giving and receiving friendly gestures while getting their coats for going home. After all the children had passed him, he rushed up with outstretched arms to give a hug. It was well returned. For several days he wanted a hug as soon as he entered the room. It was the release he needed, and the change in his work and behavior was rather dramatic. A teacher just cannot give up on a child.

Maintain Rules

You must be consistent. If basic rules are established, keep them as such. If for some reason a rule should be changed, explain it and do not pretend to not notice it. It is much better to have a few regulations that are well carried out than to have many that are partly ignored. Be consistent, but also be flexible. Sometimes, just for the fun of it, change a routine. Even having a "backwards" day, when you put the schedule in reverse, can add zest to the class activities. It can be a bit of a relaxation and fun to do something different just for the fun of it. Children like to feel that you enjoy school, too.

Maintaining even a temporary regulation can result in great benefits for a child. This can be pointed up in an experience with a recalcitrant boy who only cooperated when it suited him. The class had made applesauce and was preparing to eat it by making decorated place-mats out of paper. Joel made a few scribbles on his paper, and then cut it into small scraps. He was told quietly that this would not do, but he merely laughed and patted his scrap of paper. The children who were serving were to place the bowls only on a mat. Very soon was heard, "Hey, I didn't get a bowl." He was told there was a bowl ready and it would be served when he made a mat. Being determined to have his way, he sat and glowered while the others enjoyed their sauce, some having "seconds." When they finished, they gathered for a story. One boy could not finish his second bowl and asked to return it. Joel called, "I could eat that." He was reminded that there was a bowl ready for him as soon as he made a place-mat. When he realized that the regulation really was to be followed, with great speed he did a fairly good job of decorating a mat. He finished his applesauce just in time to get ready to leave. From that time on he showed a recognition of and respect for rules.

Children will reflect a teacher's patience, confidence, and friendly help to the extent of showing no scorn for a child with a severe handicap. A child, totally deaf and without a hearing aid, was just learning to talk. She was in a Special Education class, but she had a need for the experience of being with a larger peer group. Her problem was explained to the class before she entered. The entire group was so kind and helpful that they wanted to share, or give up, anything they were using if she was interested. Any of her attempts to communicate got smiles and praises from them. It was a wonderful experience in human loving for the class.

When a learning atmosphere and a feeling of cooperation prevail, any adult coming into the room is apt to be assumed to be a willing helper if needed. A teacher from the Special Education school was observing her pupil in the kindergarten class. She happened to be the adult not appearing to be busy. A boy working with three others at a table came to her and said, ''You better get over here. Johnny is having some trouble and needs help.'' She went over immediately and gave the needed help. The three other boys were reaching to pat timid Johnny while saying, ''See, it's all right now. You just needed help. You can do it.'' With that attitude established, children cannot help but learn and be willing to try something new.

USING THE POSITIVE INSTEAD OF THE NEGATIVE

One of the teacher's most effective tools for classroom management is the consistent use of the principles of positive reinforcement. Very simply, this means you watch for and praise the desired behavior of the children and ignore the undesirable behavior, except for extreme and disruptive actions. You do not ignore behavior which interferes with classwork or disturbs other children. This does not mean that you pretend that everything that has been done is good and give undeserved praise. Children learn to recognize such an attitude and will let their work and behavioral patterns drop accordingly. Therefore, you should establish the habit of watching for anything good that deserves attention. A quiet word of praise may be best for some; a smile or nod may be sufficient for others. You are trying to impart feelings of satisfaction by being recognized for acceptable actions. Appropriate behavior should not be ignored as just something that should have been done anyway. Some are just learning desired patterns and have a need for them to be recognized.

Children also have proper actions reinforced when they see others getting attention for those same patterns. The recognition may be a comment about how nicely some are sitting, or how well some try to do a job, or by noting how quietly a group is working.

During a free activity time, if the general noise level gets beyond what is desirable, a very helpful way to get it toned down without adding the noise of the teacher's voice is to sound the signal adopted to be used only for getting attention. When the children have stopped where they are and are looking at you, call attention to a few who are working quietly. Usually there will be some who are painting or doing something at a table which lends itself to quiet voices. Tell the class, "I have noticed something happening that is so enjoyable. I just want you to share it. Let us just have these people (the ones you want them to observe) go on with what they have been doing while we enjoy for a minute how quietly they are working." This invariably tones down the entire group. If someone is just going on his merry way, ignoring the rights of others, then he can be told privately to do some other work. If, for some reason, all continue on more of an outdoor than an indoor level of noise, and there are days when everyone seems keyed to a high pitch, they may have a need to be told that all things will be put away and a different activity will be substituted. The teacher tells them this very calmly and quietly. If she shows anger it adds to the stimulation.

When children are gathering in a group, smiling, quiet approval for those getting settled sets a pattern. Commenting on how quickly some come or how ready to listen some seem to be teaches others to have the same attitude.

Many children exhibit behavioral patterns that may not be disruptive to the group, but ones that annoy the teacher. If she calls attention to them, it merely serves as reinforcement. Imitators also may decide to try it out. Children, too, can learn to ignore some behavior as not worth watching when the teacher leads the way.

Some children have a great need for their self-image to be improved. They come to school having heard only about all the "bad" things they have done. They may have heard, "You are a bad boy (or girl)," until they believe it. Then the teacher's job of building a good self-image is even more important and it will take more time and patience. At a conference with the parents the teacher should point out that the child and his actions are two separate things. It should not be, "You are a bad boy," but, "You are a *good* boy. Why did you do that bad *thing?*" Children accept corrections willingly when they are told they are being corrected because you know what fine people they really are, and you just will not permit such fine people to do wrong things.

Point System

Group: A behavior modifier that brings good results is the point system. If one is trying to secure better behavioral patterns during a certain period, the group can earn one point a day at that specified time. There can be a chart or a place on a chalkboard designated for the point marks. When the group has earned a specified number of points they get a reward. It may be that during a conversation period there are some who disrupt. According to the situation, it may be decided that five marks earn a ten-minute period with play equipment or outdoor play. It could earn any activity the group would really enjoy. If there is a child having special difficulty in controlling himself, he may earn an extra point by himself for the group by managing his problem. This provides him with attention from his peers and encourages the others to avoid noticing his distractions. Children begin to remind each other how to cooperate in order to earn points to get to do something special.

Individually: The point system can also be very effective when used for an individual child having behavioral problems. He may be one who repeatedly interrupts during a conversation period to get attention for himself. You may set a goal for him to try to do no disturbing for five days during this period. Another child might have the habit of paying more attention to other things than his own work. He can be assigned the goal of finishing certain tasks. Prepare a small chart with spaces marked for a star each time it is earned. But do not set goals too high, for this can be discouraging to the child. The child's needs or the difficulty of attaining the goal determine the number of stars to be earned. A child having much difficulty in controlling himself needs a shorter time lapse to earn a reward. He has a need for more immediate reinforcement to develop self-control.

When the child understands his goals and knows the time period when he will be trying to earn the reward, a star is added at the end of that particular time. The child should know immediately, not at the end of the day. Even though a star is missed on one day the child can leave school feeling that he is making progress by being shown the stars he has earned. He leaves with the teacher's attitude, "Well, you missed it today, but I am sure you will make it tomorrow."

Silence: One very simple way to achieve desired attitudes requires nothing but silence. This may be done while a story is being read and quiet attention is necessary. A child's attention may stray and he might begin to talk to others. Then, without any comment, the story stops. In a short time the silence gets to the child who is distracted. He knows the story will not continue while talking is going on, and the reaction from the others causes him to become quiet.

OTHER PROBLEMS THAT COULD HINDER
THE LEARNING SITUATION

Word Concepts

Some children may be unresponsive and give the impression they are having general learning problems. It is very possible that they may have specific difficulties in basic concepts. It is not only essential for a child to understand the meanings of words, but they must be able to grasp the implications of the words when they are used in a sentence. A child may understand what the word "know" means. When he sees a picture of a boy and two houses and is asked, "Do you *know* which house is the boy's home?" he may miss the import of the word. It is easy to forget how background experiences afford such a wide divergence in word concepts, especially when they are words that are used commonly.

Tests: There are tests to check a child's concepts to disclose areas of need, enabling a teacher to teach *to* these specific needs. Mrs. Patricia Forde, as an Elementary Counselor with the Bremerton Public Schools, Bremerton, Washington, achieved productive results in diagnosing conceptual problems by using the Boehm Test of Basic Concepts, the Psychological Corporation, 1969, and the Basic Concept Inventory, Siegfried Engelmann, Follett Educational Corporation. The Basic Concept Inventory is designed for children preparing for academic tasks. It is intended for the culturally disadvantaged slow learners, emotionally disturbed, and mentally retarded. Mrs. Forde recommends using this test as soon as possible to indicate areas to which teaching should be directed. She sometimes gives the Boehm Test twice in a year to check the progress that has been made.

The Boehm Test of Basic Concepts can be given to a group of children. The Basic Concept Inventory is to be given individually.

Physical and Emotional Problems

The kindergarten teacher may be one of the first to observe physical problems that could hinder learning. Many problems, if diagnosed early, can be successfully treated. Too much delay may cause emotional and psychological factors to become involved, thus creating a much more difficult situation. This also holds true for delays in relieving sensory mode perceptual difficulties.

Dr. Richard O. Gode, Pediatrician and Child psychiatrist, Children's Psychiatric Hospital, University of Michigan, stated in a lecture to teachers doing clinical studies that "a child should first have a physical examination by a *specially trained* and *interested* physician." Further notes from his talk include:

There are signals for a teacher to be looking for and have checked—

1. Excessive fatigue.
2. Sensory input signs.
   a. Eyes: Seeing letters wrong, sight should be checked. Muscular imbalance, eye wandering especially when tired or sick. If not checked, nature takes over and vision in the lazy eye is suppressed
   b. Ears: Ear infection is frequent in young children. Look for a child not interpreting directions he should understand; tilting the head to hear.
3. Disorders of the central nervous system.
   a. Headaches most often are due to tension. Headaches that are consistent should be referred for medical attention.
   b. Personality changes that are rapid. Dramatic changes deserve attention.
   c. Head injuries should not be taken lightly. Those to the side of the head are most dangerous.
4. Seizures.
   Major convulsions are obvious. Some seizures are subtle— simply staring, especially at windows; or at fluorescent lights. If this happens in a consistent way, have it checked. Watch him at the TV. Note if his eyelids flutter during a stare, or if there is a possible head nod.
5. Behavior that might indicate an emotional problem and/or learning disability.
   a. Extreme purposeless activity—movement is nondirective, seems to be internally driven.
   b. Extremely short attention span. Can only concentrate in one-to-one situation.
   c. No control over emotions—cry, laugh, rage, too loud. Has two extremes in temper with not much in between. Is hard to discipline.

    d. Fails to learn from experience. Seems unable to retain material or recall instructions.

    e. Seems unable to learn on the abstract level, but may learn on the concrete level.

Hyperactivity: Dr. Kelleher, while associated with Olympic Center, Bremerton, Washington—a center for the emotionally and mentally handicapped—gave some suggestions for aiding hyperactive children. Included was the suggestion to make a chart for recording the time the child can work independently before he starts bouncing. When the elapsed time pattern is established, structure the setting to give him your attention just before he starts bouncing in order to break the pattern. It takes some days of observation to note the time lapses. An aide with a stop-watch can do this. The time lapse may be in seconds or minutes. The distraction, a pat, a word, or anything at the moment, should come as close in seconds as possible to stop the action immediately before it begins. This takes time at first, but gradually the undesirable action becomes suppressed and, hopefully, eliminated.

Dr. Kelleher also noted, "A threat, such as, 'You will have to stay in,' is just a gimmick and has no good value."

Have a specialist diagnose physical and emotional problems. A teacher should not act as a medical or psychological diagnostician. She should be aware of the symptoms that indicate problems and then have them checked.

CONCLUSION

The kindergarten teacher is with the children at a crucial time to observe their needs, establish good behavioral patterns, instill in the children a desire to learn, and develop in them the attitude that school is a desirable place to be.

Although a teacher cannot expect to achieve equal rapport with every child, as an adult, she must not show it. If there is a negative response and it remains constant the teacher had better look to her own approaches and attitudes.

A mutual feeling of cooperation between the parents and the teacher must be established immediately.

A book that can be used with the parents is *Living With Children*,

Gerald Patterson and Elizabeth Gullion, Research Press. In an interesting and easily understood way, it shows some errors that are commonly made when handling children. It is written to the parents, but a teacher can find good points in the book for herself.

Another excellent book is *Parents are Teachers*, Wesley Becker, Research Press. Also, *Modifying Classroom Behavior*, Hill Walker and Nancy Buckley, Research Press.

If you have resource material you can share with parents, you can help them understand that education does not stop at the school door.

DEVELOPING ESSENTIAL PERCEPTUAL-MOTOR SKILLS

3

A child's perceptual-motor ability—his recognition of body parts, body control movements, awareness of self in space relationship—is being recognized as an essential part of development to secure the needed coordination for the body patterns involved in reading and writing. Becoming skilled in motor movements aids in developing a good self-image and the confidence so essential in all learning areas. Patterns of good body movements and coordination should become fixed habits, acting as reflex actions. There should be no frustrating time delay in a thought process for hand, arm, eye or other body movements involved in any learning skill. When all body parts respond freely and easily, the processes of learning are made easier. In this chapter, you can individualize instruction with any of the exercises. Aides can be giving individual help during group exercises.

PROVEN RELATIONSHIP BETWEEN PERCEPTUAL-MOTOR ABILITY AND LEARNING

Newell Kephart was the first person to investigate perceptual-motor training. Paul Smith, Director of Assessment, Inservice, Health and Physical Education, Shoreline Public School District, Seattle,

Washington, recognized as an authority on perceptual-motor training, gave a demonstration at a reading clinic conducted by the Bremerton Public Schools in Bremerton, Washington. He stated:

> Is there unilateral control? If not, it may indicate writing problems. Is there a mixed dominance—ambidexterity—in eye, hand, or foot preference? It may indicate reading trouble. Jerky eye control tends to indicate a word-for-word reader—one who is not able to move his eyes across the words in an easy sweep. When there is a mirror action in the body, that is, the inability to immobilize one side of the body during controlled movement of the opposite side, there may be a problem in reversals. When one part of the body tends to inadvertently follow the movement of another part, the child becomes tense, resulting in poor writing. It may be necessary for this child to get up and move around periodically to relieve his tension.

Mr. Smith then gave a demonstration of the validity of his observations by using children enrolled in the clinic. Two hundred fifty children with the greatest evidence of reading difficulties had been selected for the clinical studies from 700 elementary age applicants. Their problems were being analyzed. Mr. Smith had requested three children, with parental consent, to be there for his demonstration. He had no previous knowledge of the children or their specific areas of motor skills. When the children left, Mr. Smith stated the different reading difficulties he felt were indicated by the performances made. In each case he was correct. He has repeatedly used this method in identifying difficulties.

Preventive measures rather than remedial can be taken in kindergarten. Just as delay in having organic problems diagnosed can cause emotional factors to become involved, a delay in developing good perceptual-motor abilities can find psychological and emotional problems involved that make the basic problem difficult to find.

There are various stages of perceptual-motor growth; from the motor stage you go to the perceptual stage. This includes the tactual sense, the kinesthetic, visual, auditory, form (having perception of the basic shapes), and directionality, which develops from knowing left and right. (Directionality is part motor and part perceptual.)

The conceptual stage uses motor and perceptual growth together. (Many of the activities in the chapter on visual perception are in the conceptual stage.)

Then they can, in the abstract stage, use the previous stages of motor, perceptual and conceptual to their advantage.

PRESENTING PERCEPTUAL-MOTOR EXERCISES IN THE NECESSARY SEQUENTIAL ORDER

It is well to have a guided program and to follow it explicitly. The training time is a quiet time. Children are listening and doing—*not* talking. For the end of each exercise pattern a specific signal is given, such as a whistle blown. It is important that the exercise ends in an orderly manner, having the children understand what they are expected to do at the signal. They are to stop quickly and quietly to hear whether they are to move to another exercise or put some equipment away. If they have been bouncing balls, no ball is to be bounced after the signal. If they have been jumping ropes, all jumping and rope play is to stop. This may sound structured, but it pinpoints the importance of what is being done and raises the activities well above the level of free play. Children appreciate the dignity of their efforts. Having aides walking through and assisting each child to end the activity correctly prevents the reinforcement of a poor pattern.

There is a sequential pattern to follow for proper developmental controls. It is essential that the order is followed for success. Each step should be mastered before going on to the next step. Large-muscle control is developed first, using bilateral exercises.

When that is mastered, go to the unilateral exercises where just one side—right or left—is in action. It may be just the right arm or right leg, or both, used in unison.

The third step is for the cross-lateral where one member of the right side and one on the left move smoothly at the same time. If the right arm and left leg are being extended, they should move at the same time and to the same degree.

Some activities require more space or individual direction than others. With helpers, you can divide your group, having children at different stations and rotating turns. During the exercises, mothers or older students can be of great value.

Although you are always encouraging the children with, "You're doing better," "You're getting it," "That's the way to try," do not expect them to do things not possible for them. For example, some cannot touch their toes without bending their knees. Give the direction, "See how far you can reach to the floor without bending your knees." Give them goals that are possible to reach.

EXERCISES FOR THE ROOM OR GYM
FOR INDIVIDUALS OR GROUPS

Jumping Jacks: Since right and left directionality are not involved, you may stand facing the class. Have the group positioned so that there is no interference when their arms are outstretched. If you have a gym, X marks can be taped or painted on the floor to mark where the children are to stand. Start in a standing position with arms down at the sides. At the count of "one," jump apart and the arms go out from the sides and all the way up. At the count of "two," jump back to position. The children are to move only on the count. You will note that many beginners will have difficulty jumping with their feet apart; these people will need individual help. Some children may need to practice just jumping with their feet apart for awhile. Be sure that those who are having difficulty are not criticized; encourage them for trying. Help is always given with a, "You're going to do it," attitude. Each time a child does better, let him know it. When children are working they have a need to know that their efforts and improvements are noticed. This leads to pride and further effort.

As skills develop, different children may take turns leading the group in the exercise. The importance of being a leader will make the child try harder. These ego-building experiences carry over to other activities, and the result is positive reinforcement.

Angels: Lie on the floor, arms at the sides with palms on the floor and legs together. At the command, "open," arms go out and legs spread wide; "close"—back to first position. Arms and legs should move evenly and quickly. Keep it just slow enough for a smooth movement. Help those who do not spread legs or do not move arms and legs at the same time. Some children may need more time or more individual help. Again, mothers or older students can be of great help with individuals.

Drawing Circles: Use a chalkboard. (It is also possible to tape a sheet of paper for each child on a wall.) The child holds a big piece of chalk in each fist as if he were gripping a big stick. It is not to be held in the fingers as for writing. Have him step close to the board and put his face to it. Where his nose touches, mark an "X." Then, while he keeps his head still and looks just at the X, with full arm sweeps, he makes continuous circles with both arms reaching wide and coming in before the body. He continues, without pause, making full sweeping circles. Some children will make fairly good circles; some, who will need more time, will make erratic haystacks. The sweeps should be made with a full stretch of the arms. Be sure the children do not watch their hands; they should be looking at the X. There may be a need to hold a child's head a bit so he does not turn it. One person should supervise each two or three children doing this exercise. Children will have need to pause after a shorter time than for some other exercises.

Balls: Have at least enough large-size balls to have one for every two pupils. They may bounce and catch using both hands, toss it to a partner with both hands, toss it in the air and catch with both hands, or bounce the ball to a partner.

Stepping Stones: These can be taped to the floor in a square U-shape pattern. Use a tape that adheres well and can withstand abuse. Use two colors, one for the right foot and one for the left, so they always place the foot in the square of the proper color. The opening in each square has full foot room, about six inches by eight inches, spaced to be about the distance of a normal stride apart. When a child gets to the first corner, by placing his foot in the square of the proper color, his feet will have to cross. At the second corner his feet will go back to normal walking position. Each foot is to step in the center of the space. The pattern is shown in Figure 3-1.

When skill is developed walking forward, have the class try going backwards. When the children can go forward easily, they may advance to bouncing and catching a ball with both hands each time they take a step. Bounce the ball in the empty space by the forward foot. Although stepping stones requires cross-lateral skills, the third step in progression, it can be started early.

If the floor can be marked for this exercise, children can practice it on their own.

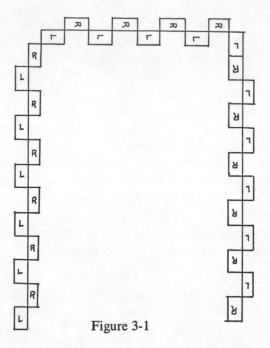

Figure 3-1

Touching Body Parts: On the direction of the teacher, children touch the head, ears, knees, shoulders, etc. with both hands (but not elbows, as this is cross-lateral).

Jumping Rope: Use ropes to jump with both feet at the same time.

Imitate Movements: The children imitate the teacher's movements. Each action uses both hands, both feet or both hands and feet. She may jump feet apart, extended arms out, up, part way out, etc.

Directionality: With both feet they jump forward, back, left, right by verbal directions. They may have a leader, with his back to them, going through the commands. Learning the left and right directions should be started early in the year.

Bunny Hop: Start in a squat position. Push forward and land on hands. Hop feet up towards hands. Repeat.

Frog: Squat with hands and feet on the floor. Spring up to have hands and feet leap forward at the same time.

Unilateral Exercises

After about one month, the group should be ready for unilateral exercises, moving just one side on command, but some may need more bilateral work on an individual basis.

Imitating Actions: In a standing position, when you say "right," you may move just the right arm or leg out, or both. The same for "left." If you demonstrate before the group, you must remember your position will be reversed when facing them. You may have a child or aide act as the leader while you watch for correct movements.

Angels: This will start in the same position as for bilateral. The commands will be "right" or "left," having only one side moving at a time. Watch for mirror action when a part on the opposite side tries to follow. Some may have a need to have arms or legs held as they try.

Crawling: Get in a crawling position—hands and knees on the floor with the back up and level; do not squat. At "right," both right hand and right knee move forward. Then "left," for the left hand and knee. After proceeding a certain distance go backwards to the start in the same way at the commands of "right," and "left."

Swimming: Lie on stomachs with the face turned to one side. The arm on that side is out from the body with the elbow bent, the palm of the hand on the floor and out from the face. The leg on the same side is extended out on the floor with the knee bent and the lower leg extending downward. The opposite arm and leg are straight down. At the command "left"—if they are facing right—the head turns to the left, the right arm and leg go straight down as the left arm and leg assume the bent position.

Side Step: Using the directions of "left, left, left," or "right, right, right," at each command of "left" the left arm extends straight out to the side as the left foot steps to the left and then the right foot closes in. The same procedure for moving the opposite way should be followed.

Left-Right: To help reinforce the knowledge of left and right directions, it can be a help to mount a large "L" in color on the left side of a wall. Put a large "R" of a different color on the right side. On the opposite wall do the same so they can see how left and right stay on the same side no matter how they face. Have them hold up a left hand and turn around to see that it is always left. While they hold up the hand, have them face another child to have them see what happens. When they learn to salute the flag, it helps them to learn the right hand. Have them face each other to shake hands with their right hands. They can look at the large letters as an aid as they move right or left, but they should get the directions established.

Up and Down Awareness: In standing position, give commands for one side of the body at a time. "With your right hand touch your right shoulder, your right knee, your right ear," etc. On command, touch with the left hand: feet, ankles, eyes, stomach, head, neck, nose, etc.

Balls: Try to bounce a ball with one hand; then the other hand. Try to toss it with one hand.

Forward Stride: Standing position. Extend right arm forward and place right foot forward. At "change" they jump up and extend left arm and foot while right side goes back.

Balance Beams: This is a cross-lateral station, but for unilateral exercise it can be used for sidestepping the same way it was done on the floor. Of course, it is much more difficult and requires constant encouragement, even when they fall off. Maybe they will only make two steps. Tell them they are getting it, or they are getting better. No negative remarks. Even if the best you can say is, "You almost made it, that's the way to try," it can be a fun time.

Cross-Lateral Exercises

As with bilateral exercises, about one month should suffice for unilateral exercises as an average. Cross-lateral has them moving one member on the right side and a different one on the left.

From a standing position at "right arm, left leg," they extend them to the side. Angels would be done the same way. You should be watching for arms or legs on the opposite side that try to follow. Sometimes the arm goes out and the opposite leg barely moves or does not move in unison with the arm. These are actions that need time and practice.

Balls can be bounced using first one hand and then the other.

Crawling can be done using right hand and left knee.

The balance beam offers good exercise walking forward, placing one foot just before the other. As skill develops, the children look straight ahead at a spot as they walk. Later they can try something more difficult, e.g., walking backwards.

Children are imaginative and enjoy pretending. You can work balance beam practice in at other times, such as for getting in line to go home. They can pretend the beam is across a stream. If they step off, their feet get wet and they must go back to have dry feet to try again.

When you are working on a circus unit, the beam can be the high wire. A record, with a good rhythm, adds atmosphere. Even the less able children imagine they are doing a very special trick and they feel pleased at what they are able to do. Of course, when you applaud their actions they assert themselves all the more. They can be animals walking on the beam by using both hands and feet.

Children can learn to turn on the beam. Practicing the turn on the floor helps. They place one foot before the other, rise on their toes and turn in the proper direction. That way they can learn to turn according to which foot is in the back. If the left foot is in back, turn to the left, and vice-versa.

Children show individual needs for perceptual-motor training in many ways. A child may show a lack of hand control. When a ball is tossed to him he may not time his grab or he may not have his two hands coming together at the same time. Another child may not be able to maintain his balance when walking along a four-inch-wide board. Some children try to hop or skip and both feet tend to move at the same time.

During a free activity time, an exercise time, or a time for games, these children can have a student or an aide help them with activities according to their needs.

ACTIVITIES FOR PERCEPTUAL-MOTOR DEVELOPMENT

Many games and exercises help to develop perceptual-motor abilities. Some are:

Chinese Sit-Up: Have the children stand in pairs back to back. Hook elbows, holding arms bent. Sit down. Then, without touching hands to the floor, stand up.

Thread the Needle: Stand. Clasp your hands in front of you. Step through your arms one foot at a time. Do not let your hands come apart when you step through the second time.

Coffee Grinder: Two children face each other. With arms spread out, they grasp hands. Turn to have the backs together. Keep turning in the same direction to face each other. Keep turning.

The Top: Stand with feet apart. Spring up, turn a quarter turn, then half, then try for a full turn. The teacher can tell them to jump around to face the wall, or whatever is in the room, to get the children to make the desired turns. They can go for one full circle on quarter turn, then half turns, and then try for full turns.

Tailer Squat: Stand with feet crossed, arms folded across the chest. Gradually lower the body to a sitting position. Return to a standing position, keeping the arms folded, by pushing from the feet.

Beanbags: Use beanbags alone or in pairs. Toss a bean bag from one hand to the other. Toss one in the air and catch it. Toss a bag to a partner. Put a beanbag on each foot and walk a given distance without having the bags fall off. This can be used as a race. If a bag falls off, stop and replace it before continuing. Put a beanbag on the head and try to walk a given distance. Try to toss the beanbags through holes in a board.

Balloons can be fun to try to keep in the air. This activity requires plenty of room.

Fox and Geese: One child is mother or father goose with three or four children behind him, each with his arms around the waist of the one in front. The mother goose holds her arms out to try to keep the fox from getting her babies. When they start, the fox faces the mother goose. The fox must run around to try to touch the last goose in the line. He may not reach under the mother's arms for the geese, but must get them by getting around to the back. The mother goose and her babies must keep turning according to the way the fox goes. The "babies" in the line must move to stay behind the mother. A fox can get the first one or two quickly, and they leave the line as they are touched. It becomes difficult to get the last one.

There are also animal walks that demand coordination—

The Duck Waddle: Squat on your heels—do not just bend over.

Feet must be spread apart. With hands on shoulders the arms become wings, or hands may be placed at the waist. Then, keeping feet flat on the floor, waddle from side to side. The knees soon get tired from this position, so the walk should not last too long.

Dog Walk: Hands and feet on the floor—walk. Lame dog! Hold one foot up while walking with two hands and one foot.

Elephants: Children must think and feel "big." Hands and feet on the floor. Slowly right hand and right foot advance. Then the left side. This is a unilateral exercise.

Rowing Boats: Two children sit facing each other. Bend the knees and touch the feet together. Grasp hands and row back and forth. A longer rowing sweep may be gotten by having each child place one leg between the legs of the other child. This should be done with music or a rhythmic command.

Some of the games suggested in the section on visual perception are also motor-training exercises. Group dances also provide good motor exercises: "Did you Ever See a Lassie" requires duplicating the actions of the child in the center; "Here We Dance Looby Loo" involves left and right directions, as does "Hokey-Pokey."

Crossing the Brook: A space is marked on the floor to be the brook. If it is narrow, the children may try a standing jump to cross the brook so as not to get their feet wet. When the space becomes wider they may take a run before the jump.

Hop, Step, and Jump can be used in the room. One child at a time holds one foot up for a big hop. Then he tries to reach out from where he landed with as long a step as he can make. He puts his feet together, swings his arms, and jumps as far as he can. Mark the spot and have another child try.

Wheelbarrow Racing: One child is on his hands. A partner steps between his lower legs and grasps him by the knees. They try to race around an object and back to the starting point.

Rocking Chairs: Children lie flat on the floor face down, arms extended in front. Raise arms, heads, and legs. They try to rock on their tummies.

Ball Bat: Batting balls is a good game and exercise that can be prepared from materials you can collect. Materials needed are wire coat hangers, old nylon stockings and small Styrofoam balls. Pull the coat hangers to form a long triangle. Then bend up the hook to form a sort of handle. ⊂▭ Cut the foot from a stocking and tie a knot. Slip it over the hanger to stretch tight. Wrap the top of the stocking around the wire handle and either tie it or stitch it. This makes a good bat for the balls. The balls are so light they do not hurt anything when they hit, and they can be used in the gym or outdoors to provide good running and swinging exercise.

Touch Box: For tactile experiences, have a box with a variety of objects in it: comb, pen, glasses, wood, sponge, eraser, cotton, fur, pin, string, velvet, sandpaper, etc. One way to use it is in a group situation. One child draws out an object while his eyes are covered. He tries to identify the object by touch. Another way to prepare the box is to have it sealed. Cut two holes for the hands, one on either side. A child reaches into the box, feels an object and names it before he takes it out to verify his guess. The box can be on the science table to be used by individuals or in small groups to see which child can correctly name the most objects.

Feely: You can have books or sets of ''feely things'' for them to look at while they handle the objects.

You can put the same textured materials on two boards. After a child has felt the materials while seeing them, he tries to match pieces on the two boards while being blindfolded.

Have a child close his eyes. Touch one part of his arm. Have him tell you where you touched. Then touch his arm twice. Have him tell where.

Secret Message: The ''Secret Message'' is a conceptual game which is also enjoyable. It can be used while learning shapes, numerals, or letters. A child faces the chalkboard. With your finger, you carefully draw the shape on his back between his shoulders. He then tries to reproduce it on the board. The group watches to see if he got your secret message. This also helps with directionality. If someone starts to reproduce the message in reverse, draw it again, slowly, on his back. A few may have a need to feel it while they reproduce it.

Body parts: For kinesthetic experiences, call out the parts of the body as the children respond by touching them. Then go faster and faster until it is not possible to keep up. This game usually ends in relaxed laughter. Another—to the tune of "Here We Go Round the Mulberry Bush"—is:

"My head, my shoulder, my knees, my toes, (touching parts as sung)
My head, my shoulders, my knees, my toes,
My head, my shoulders, my knees, my toes,
We all grow strong and tall."

The second time start with shoulders,

"My shoulders, my knees, my toes, my head,
My shoulders, my knees, my toes, my head,"

Continue the verses until the last one starts:

"My toes, my head, my shoulders, my knees," etc.

Have arrow cards pointing up, right, left, and down, for them to imitate. Use the cards one at a time or bilaterally. Use over, under, above, below, in directions for them to follow. They can do this with their bodies or hands. Or use pipe-cleaner men to be placed over, under, by, on, in, using a small box for placement.

Hand Muscles: To develop hand muscles, give sheets of newspaper torn in quarter size. See if they can crumple it with just one hand holding the paper in the air, not pressing on anything. Use the dominant hand.

For small-muscle control, have children fold a paper and try to make lines within the fold following the fold directions.

Put a small circle on a paper. See if they can use different colored crayons to make increasingly larger circles around it.

To develop motor control, you can use dotted lines for the children to trace with their fingers. Then use a crayon. Frostig and Lippincott have some special tracing exercises; you can also make your own.

You can draw a simple maze for them to trace with their finger and then stay in the path with a crayon.

Visual: Motor and visual perceptions work together. Have a child lie down; then draw around him and cut out the shape, or use a figure cut-out. Have them show the right arm or leg according to the way the figure is turned. Each child may have a small figure with movable parts. Directions can be given to move the right arm up. Move the left leg out. Move the left arm and right leg out.

When you are having perceptual-motor training it is best to have a gym and some extra help to have small groups working at different areas at a time, some for jumping jacks or angels, some on the balance beam, some at the stepping stones, others at a chalkboard making circles. After a few minutes they rotate to the next station. Mothers can serve as aides in this type of situation, and some high schools have programs for students to share their time helping in grade schools.

Two excellent books dealing with perceptual-motor training are:

Roach, Eugene G., and Kephart, Newell G. *The Perdue Perceptual-Motor Survey*. Charles E. Merrill Books, Inc., 1966.

Smith, Paul. *Neuromuscular Skills for Assisting Neurophysiological Maturation*. Shoreline Public Schools, WA, 1967.

TECHNIQUES TO ACHIEVE MEANINGFUL VISUAL RESPONSES

4

A child must have good visual responses if he is to experience successful learning, and much can be done for children's perceptual abilities through training. While training visual responses you will also be incorporating motor activities, auditory and oral training. Sight is physical; vision is trained.

Background experiences will enter into the picture. Does the child perceive what is there or does previous experience, or lack of experience, cause lack of observation? Children with rich backgrounds of books, pictures, and someone's interest in helping them be aware of all that is around have a decided advantage in being able to respond intelligently. In this chapter you can individualize instruction with all of the activities other than those indicating the need for group participation, such as "Sit and Say." Again, these activities can all be done with the use of teacher aides.

RECOGNIZING VISUAL PROBLEMS THAT HINDER LEARNING

From the start, a teacher should try to observe in her students any apparent physical difficulties in vision. Such obvious things as squinting or turning the head to favor one eye are indications that a checkup is in order. It is also well for school districts to administer checkups for amblyopia, a disease which can cause serious impairment to vision if left untreated.

An example of evidence for visual help could be a child's not being able to recognize the numerals 1, 2, 3, no matter how many times or ways they may have been presented. If games have been tried repeatedly with numbers, matching them, saying them, matching the numerals with sets of objects or objects with the numerals, and then a ''3'' is shown and the child guesses ''6'' or any other number, you are getting a strong signal: ''I need individual help.'' It is possible that the child needs treatment for actual visual impairment; but if the eyes are in good physical order, he may need perceptual training. Sight is a physical thing; for vision, there are learned skills.

When the physical condition of the eyes has been assured the teacher must become aware of any *visual* problems. Can the child recognize differences between colors or shapes? Can he match shapes visually? Can he recognize differences in sizes? Can he find missing parts of an object or tell what objects logically go together? Does he remember objects seen and in the order in which they were seen?

The following discussion will cover some eye-muscle exercises, then visual perceptual problem areas with exercises to develop the areas involved.

EXERCISES TO DEVELOP THE IMPORTANT EYE MUSCLES

The eyes are controlled by muscles and these muscles need to be exercised. Especially important is the need for an easy left-to-right sweep when reading.

Here are a few exercises to be used for conditioning of the eye muscles:

1. Lie on the floor. Keep your head still. Find the clock with your eyes. Now look at the windows, only moving your eyes (or whatever will sweep the eyes from one side to the other).
2. Sit straight. Hold your arms straight out from you and make fists with your thumbs held up. Keep your head still. With your eyes

look at your left thumb, then your right thumb. Spread your arms apart a bit and try it. Spread farther. See how far you can spread your arms and still see your thumbs without moving your head.

3. An eye exercise to get a full movement from side to side is to make cut-out objects such as a frog on a cardboard holder and a lily pad to be at the opposite side, and to have the frog "hop" to it. Or you could cut out a ball and have a basket picture or a mitt to catch the ball. Then you would tell the children, "See this ball I have. I am going to toss it right into the basket. I want your eyes to follow the ball, but be very sure your head does not move. Just your eyes follow the ball." Or have the frog hop to the lily pad. Use this exercise individually.

4. Have a ball hanging on a string. Swing the ball from side to side. The eyes follow it without moving the head.

5. For left-to-right movement, put shapes (or numerals, if learned) on the board: one set on the left, one set on the right, each shape a different color. Have them say the first one on the left, then the first one on the right. An example of an easy beginning way could be: left side—red circle, green triangle, yellow rectangle, blue square; right side—red square, green circle, yellow triangle, blue rectangle. Tell them, "Say the name of the red shape on the left. Without moving your head let your eyes find the red shape on the right. What shape is it?" Continue with the other shapes, reminding the children to hold their heads still. This type of activity can be used for vertical eye movement also.

INDIVIDUALIZED INSTRUCTION AND GROUP ACTIVITIES TO DEVELOP VISUAL PERCEPTION

Children who have special needs for visual training often make their needs evident. They may display difficulties in the following tasks:

1. Color discrimination;
2. Seeing the differences in shapes, whether geometric or objects;
3. Recalling the shapes or objects seen;
4. Recalling the order of shapes and being able to make a fair copy;
5. Perceiving directionality—whether the shape directs right, left, up, or down;
6. Noticing details.

There is much use of recall as visual training and memory training go hand in hand. Some difficulties may stem from a need for memory training.

Color Perception

Matching Colors: Children should master shapes and color awareness early in their learning. Since traffic safety is a must, when they first come to school the red, green and yellow round shapes furnish a natural start. The auditory sense can aid the visual with poems such as:

> *Red is for stop,*
> *Yellow means slow.*
> *Wait for the green,*
> *Then we go.*

Match the colors with other colors in the room. Children may find the colors on their clothes.

A child who has special problems recognizing colors can be given certain color chips plus a box of multi-colored paper scraps or pieces. He is to find the colors in the box to match his chips. Working with an aide, he can be told the name of one color and then try to find several pieces of that color. Again, the aide can put out several pieces, each of two or three colors, and have the child find a color as requested. To afford some action, which adds incentive, the child can be told to find a color in as many places in the room as he can. Of course, the aide must understand that a child having difficulties needs praise and encouragement, not only for success, but for effort.

Sit and Say: A favorite group game is called "Sit and Say." The colors are put on the floor. One child hides his eyes; another sits on a color and then says "ready." The first child asks, "Are you sitting on _____?" (This is just another place to get questions and answers in sentences.) As colors are learned they are added. This game is also used for numerals, and it aids in recall as well as discrimination of colors.

Color Tag: Another game, very much enjoyed for its action, is "Color Tag." While one child hides his eyes a colored paper about four inches across is pinned on the back of another. Without touching, the first child tries to get around to see the color while the second child tries to turn to keep him from seeing it.

Form Constancy

Learning shapes should start early. Work on one. Match it with others as to size or color. Find the same shape in objects in the room. Find it in a collection of shapes. Trace it in the air. Draw objects of that shape. Draw balloons, cookies, wheels, etc. Proceed to the next shapes—square, triangle, and rectangle. Do this individually or in a group, according to the children's needs.

A fun game after the shapes have been introduced is to have many sizes and colors of the four shapes cut from construction paper. Pass them out, one to a child. Then ask all the children having round shapes to stand, then those having square shapes, etc. Then call out colors, and finally, be more specific, such as round red shapes, green triangles, yellow and blue rectangles. When you notice a child having problems, give him individual help.

Visual form perception can be used with three-dimensional objects. You can work with categories. The following are good for individual use:

Show me the round things in the room; the square wooden things; the red things; the things that move.

It can be more specific:

Find a particular picture (by your description), a toy, a vase, getting less and less conspicuous.

Sort objects as to shape, color, use, size.

You may have cubes, spheres, three- and four-sided pyramids. Separate them as to size, color, texture.

Hold up a block, find another like it.

Matching shapes: Ditto a paper of shapes. Then give out pre-cut shapes to match on the first sheet. This can also be a seasonal activity. You can have apples, Christmas trees, hearts, etc., in various sizes to match.

Spin the Pointer: A dial can be made with a variety of shapes around the edge. Spin the pointer. Say the shape where the pointer stops. If you make a sturdy dial you can use slip-over sheets for numerals, colors, or whatever.

Fishing: Cut tagboard fish that vary in size, form, color, and details, but have at least two of each. The fish have a hole punched at the head with a paper fastener put in. A magnet is tied to a string on a stick to catch the fish. The game is to see if with two casts, they can match a pair. If not, one is put back and the children continue to try to match the fish. The one matching the most wins. Two children can play.

Have shapes with directionality; this could be a pointed triangle or the **E** shape. Place them so they point different ways. Then ask a child to find the one pointing left, right, up, or down; or have a row of shapes with one or two pointing a different way. Find the one that does not belong.

Visual Recall

As recognition of shapes is acquired, the children can learn to copy them. Shapes can be traced in the air after you have shown them, one at a time, to the class. Children can use templates. You may have metal templates, or you can cut a square from cardboard and cut out a shape in the center. Use larger sized templates at the chalkboard. Have them draw by following the inner edge shape. When a child seems ready, have him try to draw without the template. If this proves too difficult, have him use the template once more. Practice on paper with smaller templates, and have children finger-trace shapes on paper and then try to make their own.

Recognizing shapes: Draw a circle and show a circle cutout. Have the children try to draw one. If they are way off, let them use a cardboard cutout to trace with their fingers until a fair copy can be made. When one is mastered, go to the next shape. Introduce sizes—big, little, larger, etc., so the meaning of the terms are learned as they see them.

Show rows of ten geometric shapes varied in shape and color.

Are all the squares red? Find a square that is not red.

Are all the red shapes square? Find a red triangle, a red round shape. Find the blue triangle. Find the square shapes, etc.

Recalling shapes: Give out paper with a row of shapes down the left side. Have them make some of their own on the right side of the paper. Begin with simple shapes (Figures 4-1 and 4-2).

Use a paper of shapes that have completed shapes on the left. The shapes on the right are to be finished to be like the completed shapes. As their individual skills develop, offer more complicated patterns, but do not add the more complicated shapes until a child can master the simple ones (Figures 4-3, 4-4, 4-5, and 4-6).

Have a paper of shapes for the children to observe the shape on the left, and then find the shape on the right that matches it (Figure 4-7).

Use "Please Finish Me" pictures (Figure 4-8).

Some children have difficulty retaining a mental image of a line or

Figure 4-1

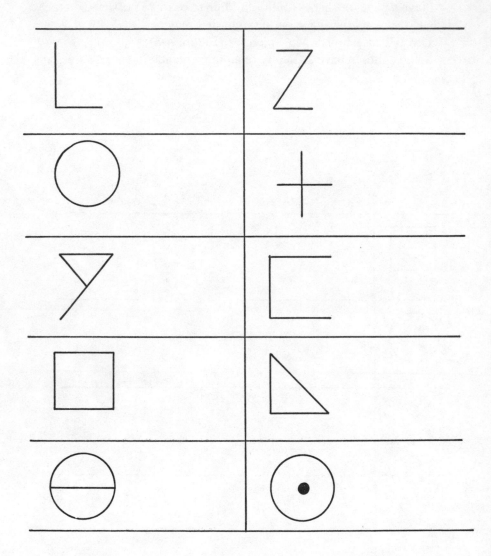

Figure 4-2

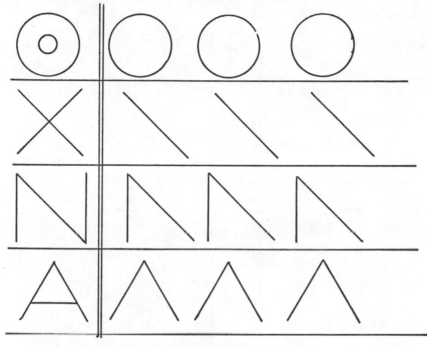

Figure 4-3

shape for the time it takes the eyes to move from left to right. They must begin with easy images for success.

Another good exercise is to make sets of shapes on flash cards, from easy sets to more difficult ones. Position the children where they can all see the shape at the same angle and time (or do it individually). One way is to have them use their chairs as tables, kneeling in front of their chairs. Hold up one shape at a time. Give directions to look at the shape all the while it is held up as it will not be shown after you put it down. The children are to look at the shape for about five seconds. Then put it down and have them make a copy. When the set is finished, show the shapes again, one at a time, to have the children check their work. Remember, it is observation we are trying to develop, not who did the best. Do not criticize mistakes, but individually show what the errors may have been. Then try again and praise the children for their efforts. As this skill grows, the shapes become more detailed (Figures 4-9 and 4-10).

Use flash cards that are about 6″ x 6″. Use each set more than one

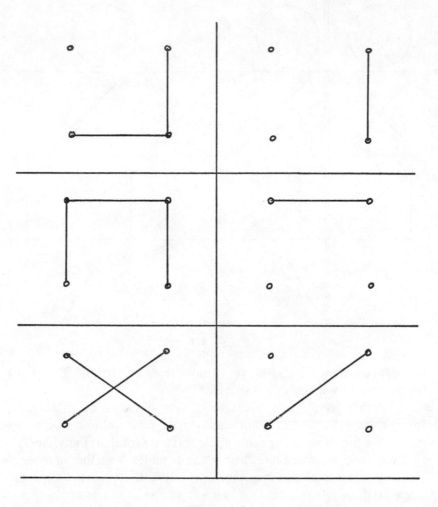

Figure 4-4

time and turn the cards that have directional lines or shapes. Caution the children to observe the direction of the lines as they may not be pointing the way they were when the cards were seen before. When a shape has been difficult for a child to duplicate in a reasonable way, hold the card by his drawing so that he may see the direction or the numbers of lines, and how his is different. Guide him to notice the direction of the lines before a second attempt is made. When the children make a "one" on

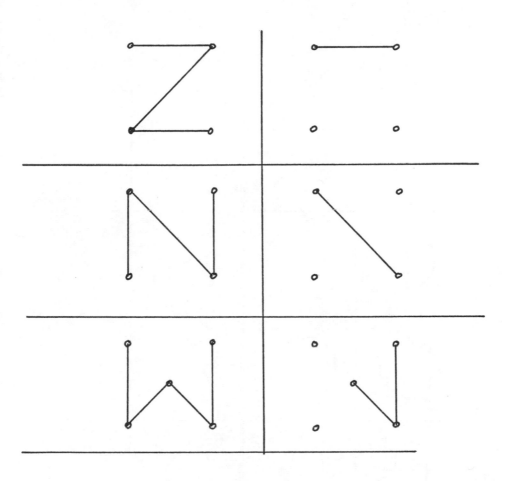

Figure 4-5

the paper for their first attempt, and then put a "two" on the other side for the second try, you can check on improvement when you review the work.

Another way to train recall of shapes individually is to hold up a card with a shape for about three seconds—less time as they become skilled. Then: "Name what you saw"; "make what you saw in the air"; "pick it out" (from a set of shapes on a strip); "make one like it."

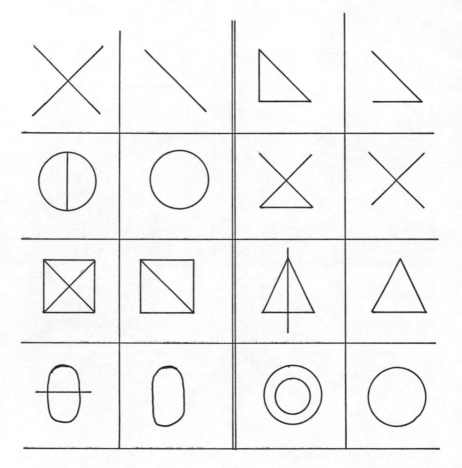

Figure 4-6

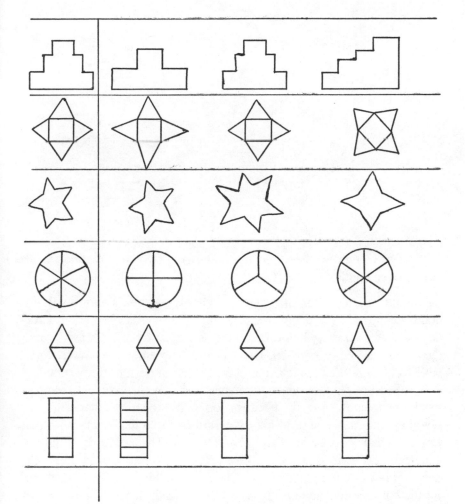

Figure 4-7

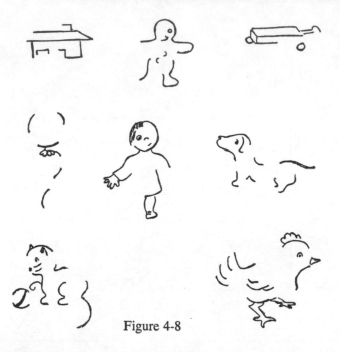

Figure 4-8

After using one shape, go on to showing two shapes, one shape drawn over another.

Names: During the first week of school, children's names will no doubt be printed for many uses. Using name cards on tagboard for attendance can be very helpful, and this is a boon for substitutes. When the names can be recognized, have the cards spread out each day on a table for the children to pick up and bring to your desk as they come in.

When you first introduce the name cards, show some that are very much the same to show the need for looking at the whole name. For a few days let each one hold his own card to trace the letters with his fingers. Then choose a few cards at a time to hold to see if those children can find their own. Praise them for success. As more are reading their names, choose more cards to put where you will eventually have them for the children to find to bring to your desk as they come in each day. Some children will be ready to copy their names on their own papers.

Pictures offer good recall exercises. Show a picture to be observed for several seconds. Then put the picture aside and have a child recall as much as he can about the picture. When he can recall no more, another

Figure 4-9

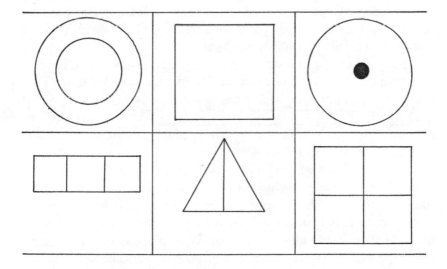

Figure 4-10

may try to see if something was omitted. The picture should be fairly simple for first attempts. Gradually bring out others with several objects or more details. With practice, many children gain the skill of observing and recalling not only the main subjects, but much of the detail.

Sometimes there is a need for a device to spark the desire to recall what is perceived. One that is fun to use is Willie the Worm. Cut many brown circles about 2" in diameter. On some, draw Willie's face.

 When a child can read the numeral or letter needed and write it on direction, he may put it on a circle that gets stapled to Willie. The children enjoy watching Willie grow.

Visual Sequential Memory

When you think about the words children must learn, the importance of sequential memory is obvious. Do they immediately recall saw or was? Or the letters TAR—as in rat, art, or tar?

Beads: Simple bead stringing can grow to following a set pattern. Have a box or bag of beads with a card having four beads mounted in a pattern. This can be a good drawing of four beads. The child is to copy the pattern and continue it. When the children are able to do this they may make their own pattern and repeat the procedure.

Building blocks: Blocks are handy and good for use as patterns. Arrange a set in an easy pattern. Have a child copy it. Then see if he can remember the pattern without seeing it.

For a group situation when working on logical sequences, have the group in a circle. Start a block pattern. Then let each child in turn add the next logical block. When the first easy pattern has been a success—such as ☐ ☐ ☐ ☐ ☐ ☐ —add to and complicate the pattern. You must do two units of the pattern so the children understand what is to follow.

Always work with praise for proper choice. Even when you have four different shapes going in a pattern, the slowest will have a feeling of success if the group has learned patience. If a child is not sure which block to choose, help in a friendly way by repeating the pattern with him from the start. The auditory sense works with the visual. Even some who happened to guess correctly will show understanding and relief while you are chanting long, short, round, triangle, over and over. When the child being helped gets the correct one, he will be reinforced if you say, "I knew you could," especially so when the group shows approval for correct responses.

The block activity can be used with flannel board shapes or cutout shapes in the same way for individual help.

Letter shapes: While learning abstract shapes the children can also recognize the differences in letter shapes. They can recognize upper- and lower-case differences. They can learn the general letter groupings in names and words used in the room. Label objects in the room. Some get to recognize the words. Some get to know the beginning sound.

Make cards with pairs of upper-case letters. Make another set with lower-case letters. Pair up letters that are very different, such as **GH, rt;** then have some that are not too different, such as **BD, mn.** Have some only different in directionality, as with **bd.** Have some the same. Show them one at a time and have the children say "the same," or "different." To keep them attentive to the exercise, you can at times ask the group, "do you agree?" Use upper-case letters for one session, lower-case for another.

Later you can show groups of letters: **EFE OOO OQO MMN** etc. Or lower case: **mmn pbp bbb dbb** etc.

Later you can have a card with two sets on it to tell whether the sets are alike or different. Have some in reverse order to show the need for left-to-right eye movement. When an individual is having difficulties seeing the reversed sets, have the groupings on separate cards. Then the child can place one above the other so he can better see and understand the letter positions.

GQ—QG   IL—IL   MM—MW
ec—eo   dbd—pbp   MON—MON

Have some letters the same, some different. Keep the pressures off. Do not let a child get "shook" over an error, and by all means praise correct responses.

The kinesthetic approach, when body movements create sensory impressions, strengthens the visual sense. There are wooden letters to handle; sandpaper letters can be felt; white glue can be made into letter forms to make good rigid letters to cut out and feel. A double tracing of the letter with glue with about ¼" between lines is an easy way to make them. Of course, numerals can be used the same way.

In the fall, if you plan a party such as an applesauce party to celebrate harvest time, the children can make place-mats. On 12" x 18" construction paper, have them arrange a border of pre-cut apples in three colors, using a repeat pattern. This teaches them to form patterns with a purpose.

Individual sequential memory training: To help those children having visual-sequential memory difficulties, a set of chips with a shape or form on them is good to use. (These shapes can be dittoed and cut out.) Arrange a few chips in an order. Allow the child about five seconds to study it. Then mix them and have the child duplicate. Always start with an easy arrangement to assure immediate success and confidence. For a child with weak sequential memory, it could be ◯ Ⓐ ◯ Ⓐ . When the child masters this, you might go to ◯ Ⓐ Ⓐ ◯ Ⓐ Ⓐ . Then add a third type of chip.
Another individual aid is to use hand signals to have the child imitate. Hold up one finger for about two seconds. Put your hand down and have the child imitate your action. Hold up both hands with one finger on each hand up. The child imitates. Hold up one hand with two fingers up, then hold up one, pause, then two fingers. Have the child repeat this sequence.
Arrange some objects in order; start with two or three. The child tries to duplicate this procedure. Go slowly to add different objects; you can change the order of the objects. Later, make the difference more subtle by adding a different color, or one with a missing part.

Visual Constancy

Place an object before a child. This could be one block, a ball, a book, a jar, etc. Place others of the same shape but in a variety of sizes at a distance. Find one the same size.
Stack blocks at one point and then stack others at a distance. Which stack is the same? Prove it.
Provide pictures of blocks. Pick out the correct block for each shape and make a simple block structure. The child indicates a corresponding picture. Try to build to duplicate.
Draw a body on the board. Touch a part of the drawing. A child touches another child at the same part and names it.
Draw partially completed faces and figures. Children finish them for you. This is also used with the ''Please Finish Me'' exercise.

Visual Interpretation and Discrimination

Select objects by color, shape, or use, and use them to introduce categories. This can be developed further by having an aide use them on a one-to-one basis.

With the children in a circle, put out a large assortment of objects on the floor. Have children group them as to which objects they think should go together. They may group them as to color, shape, composition or use. Accept their category and have them explain why each was chosen. You may decide the type of selection.

Visual interpretation and reasoning to hand-in-hand in areas where perception is involved. There are other suggestions for category development in the chapter on reasoning.

Show small sets of shapes—one, two, three, four squares. Try to recognize the number of shapes without having to count each one.

Show sets of shapes and determine which has the most and which has the least. Let the differences between sets be obvious so the children can recognize them, and then prove their conclusions by counting. Eventually, they will learn to see objects in groups and, without counting, to rationalize which groups have the most objects in them.

Provide them with objects in various sizes in a mixed arrangement. Let them indicate which are the same size without measuring them. These objects can be cutout letters or numerals, as well as other shapes.

Show a shape with a cutout piece missing. Then have cut shapes for them to choose the missing piece.

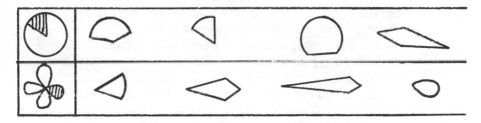

Use shapes cut in pieces. Cut a square from corner to corner. Cut a rectangle in half. See if the children can fit shapes together to make a square or a rectangle.

Being able to see *intelligently* is of vital importance. When the teacher is satisfied that other physical needs are cared for she can work on the development of visual skills. The needs of the group will vary. Some children will need one-to-one help, and they each must feel success to be able to go ahead to the next step.

The worksheets that follow are merely suggestions. The children must have good visual perception and understand the basic steps or they will become more confused and experience feelings of failure when given material that is beyond them. However, repeated use of easy materials can also bore those who are capable of doing advanced work.

DEVELOPING VISUAL PERCEPTION THROUGH GAMES

1. Sit and Say—(explained in text, color discrimination)
2. Color Tag—(explained in text, color discrimination)
3. Did You Ever See a Lassie?—(imitating body movements, constancy)
4. Lost Child—Done different ways:
   One child leaves his usual place. Who is gone? (recall) Or, describe a child. Find the one described. He may be the one to do the finding next. (recall, constancy, discrimination)
5. "I'm Thinking Of"—Use some nonidentifying names. (Good for visual recall, constancy and interpretation.) They ask only descriptive questions such as the color of his hair, his shoes, etc. If a child guesses a name and it is wrong he can't guess again. Much identification may be necessary.
6. What is Missing?—(recall, constancy)
   Have a tray of objects or group of objects on the floor. One turns around. Remove an object. Tell what is missing.
7. Fishing—(recall, constancy, interpretation)
   Have a box of shapes, letters, colors, etc. with paper fasteners and a fishing pole with a magnet. "Fish" for two that match.
8. Lotto Game—(constancy)
   Cards passed out with the diagram: . They have envelopes of shapes in color. Draw shapes from the envelope. They must match a row of shapes and color.
9. Travel Game—(discrimination, constancy)
   Have a set of city name cards using colored cardboard. Use the same color for each of two cities—such as two yellow cards for New York and Disneyland, two orange cards for Los Angeles and Chicago, etc. Then have two matching ticket cards in the same colors with the city name on them. Arrange the city

names around the room. Let some draw the tickets. At the signal "fly," children try to locate their destination. They match by color and name. (This is further described in Chapter 8.)

10. There are sets of pictures to buy that call for close examination. Some are quite inexpensive. They come in duplicate sets of shapes or pictures requiring fine discrimination. (discrimination, constancy)

11. Domino Sets (discrimination)
They can be used as a game or matching pairs.

12. Many lotto games are available. Some match same pictures, related pictures, or missing parts. (interpretation, constancy, recall)

13. Pictures—(recall, constancy)
Have sets of pictures such as Halloween, Fall, Thanksgiving, etc. Have label cards near the pictures for a few days, such as pictures of a ghost, a pumpkin, and a witch with name labels. Then see who can match a duplicate set of name cards with the ones by the pictures. Very capable children will match name cards with just the pictures.

14. Have pictures of "My Favorite Story." Try to guess. (recall, interpretation)

15. A Game for 4 Children—(constancy)
Have a bag with about 50 beads in it. Each child draws out six without looking. Try to match the beads they drew as to color and shape. They draw in turns. The first one to have all his beads matching wins. The second draw is limited to two beads. It could be decided to have the child with the most pairs matched being the winner when all were drawn, or they could put back the unmatched beads after each drawing. Another way is, on the second drawing, to put back one bead not matched before drawing two more.

16. Sitting in a Circle—(recall, constancy)
Place a set of objects on the floor. Enumerate them. Then have one child turn away. Remove one object. The child then looks back and tries to tell which object is missing. After several turns change some of the objects to make it more interesting for those having later turns. This game can go quite quickly so all can get turns.

17. Games for Recall
Have five or six children stand in a row. After one child observes them and turns away, one child in the row leaves. Who

is gone? A variation is to put different hats on the row of children. Then, while one is not watching, have two exchange hats. Which ones have different hats?

The same idea is easily used with pictures. Arrange the pictures in some order. Observe them for a short time. While the group cannot see, rearrange the pictures. Who can put them back as they were?

A memory game that is more difficult, and a challenge, is to have five children in a row facing the group. Give each of the five a numeral card to hold in order, 1 to 5. Have the group study the line to recall each child holding a given number. Then collect the cards and say "scramble." The five then quickly move about and end by facing the watching children in some different order. Have some child try to return the same card to the child who held it in the first position. It is not easy!

TRAINING FOR
AUDITORY SKILLS

5

Some children process information more efficiently by one sensory mode than by another. There is a need to be alert to their sensory strengths and weaknesses and have teaching techniques appropriate to auditory, visual or kinesthetic sensory needs. Research indicates a need for more emphasis on auditory training, especially sequential memory skills.

The first need is to note and check physical problems. Some children, having no physical difficulties, have developed habits of hearing sounds while applying no mental effort to sort them out or to relate them in any way to past experiences. Some children have had so much purposeless talking directed at them that they have adjusted themselves to ignore general conversation. For some, there may have been no reason to listen or to try to remember because they have experienced so much repetition, such as directives that were not followed through. They may have lacked having an adult share ordinary conversation with them. (It should be "with" them and not "at" them.) It becomes the obligation of the kindergarten teacher to develop purposeful listening. When the children have learned to listen with a reason, their ability to retain what has been heard in sequential order can be developed. Then they may proceed to the level of listening for sounds, so necessary in pre-reading.

In kindergarten there is a unique opportunity and responsibility to develop a child's ability to listen and process what is heard efficiently. There must be effort made to develop a relationship between what he hears and what he experiences. There must be training to develop the ability to recall what has been heard in the order heard.

In this chapter you can individualize for the slower child by using "Hearing sounds," "Matching sounds," "Series of numbers," "Arranging objects," "Rhythmic patterns," "Physical patterns," "Repeating a story," "Recalling objects," and "Rhyming words."

For the bright child, use "Classifying sounds," "Matching sounds" (they will be able to match more sounds), "I went to the store," "Acting a story," and "Rhyming words." They can also use "Recalling objects" with more objects or objects of finer detail.

EASY WAYS TO SPOT HEARING DIFFICULTIES

The lack of physical hearing can be a subtle thing. Some children with poor hearing have adapted their reactions from early childhood. It may be difficult to spot them without tests. They may have taught themselves to read lips and expressions. There have been cases of children being classed as mentally retarded from infancy, when the difficulty was that of deafness. Ear infections in young children can be very common. They may come and go. Children with this problem usually respond normally, but on some days show a lack of response. Many times a nonconformer just hasn't heard the directions. As with sight, there is a physical side to sound perception that may need medical attention.

Audiometer tests are a real asset. They should be administered by a person who is skilled. Some pediatricians use an audiometer; some speech therapists use them. Some school systems have a trained person going around to all the schools testing hearing. Sometimes one ear may not be working and the child's best response position can be noted. Notice the children who tend to turn one ear toward the direction of sounds. Check questionable cases by holding a watch near an ear to note if one ear is not hearing well. Some do not receive high pitch frequency sounds. They may not hear the words from a voice with a high pitch, but be able to understand when a voice has a low pitch. Some tend to lean forward to hear. As soon as a teacher has become sufficiently acquainted with her group to note listening habits and attitudes, it is well to have tests for those with questionable attitudes. If the school does not provide the service, it would be worth the effort of the parents to have a pediatrician check the hearing.

Classroom Games

There are some simple games that may indicate hearing difficulties. One is to have the children standing in a circle with their hands behind their backs. One child sits in the center and, with eyes closed, pretends to be asleep. Another child tip-toes around on the outside of the circle and puts into someone's fingers a short string that has a jingle bell tied on the end. When the child returns to his place in the circle he says, "Bo-Peep, your sheep are missing," or, "Santa, your reindeer has gone," (or use some other seasonal topic). Show how the one with the bell can just move his fingers to jingle the bell to avoid any arm movement. The one in the center must locate the direction of the sound as the bell rings, and then go to the child he thinks has the bell and ask, "Do you have my sheep (my reindeer)?" If that child does not hold the bell he just answers, "No, I do not have ——." The bell goes on jingling until its sound is located. The bell is not loud. The child must hear the direction of the sound. You might note a head turned one way or another to hear. Some children may have no idea of the sound's direction. Occasionally one with hearing difficulties will not hear the bell at all. These children should have their hearing tested.

Another circle game for fine hearing is to have one child in the center with eyes covered. The group, holding hands, walks around singing or chanting, "I'm very, very tall" (as they stretch up), "I'm very, very small" (as they walk stooped over). "Sometimes tall," (stretch high), "Sometimes small," (stooped down), "Guess what I am now." On the last line they are all stretched or stooped according to the teacher's lead. The one in the center tries to tell by the voice direction whether they are tall or small.

SIMPLE, FUN WAYS TO DEVELOP PURPOSEFUL LISTENING

There are many activities that give a good reason for listening and enhance listening skills. They offer a challenge and create an interest in what is happening. Without any interest or desire to hear, very few sounds, especially those of the voice, will make much impression. Listening must be more than a passive happening. There must be enough motivation or purposeful action for the minds to be actively involved. The habit of just hearing sounds and letting the mind wander is an easy one to acquire when bored. Too much talking by the teacher tends to create a nonlistening habit in the children. The teacher must assure turns for children's talking time. There must be quiet times if there are to be listening times. The noise level in the room should generally be low. There must also be assurance that the vocabulary used is understood.

Teaching by Making Mistakes

Learning poems: It is easy to hold interest when the teacher has the children trying to catch her in a mistake. If a poem is being taught, it can be told once or twice. Ask some questions about it to be sure the main points and words were understood. Then tell them you will say it again, but this time you will make some mistakes; they are to let you know when you make a mistake and also be ready to tell what you should have said. For example, if they are learning Little Boy Blue, for the first line you might say, "Little Boy Green." Someone will immediately signal with his hand and give the correct response. After a, "good for you," say the first line correctly and possibly go on with something silly for a laugh to perk up any lagging interest, such as, "Come blow your nose." They love to laugh with the teacher at her mistake. Then, when that has been corrected, say the first two lines correctly and make a mistake in the next one. Each time praise their good listening, and repeat correctly all the lines previously said. By the time they have heard the last line, and have corrected it, they have had good reason to listen to the entire poem several times and will have it learned. Do not permit children to call out responses, as some would never get a turn. Of course, if you let them know you might be sneaky, you might slip in another mistake in the middle to check their listening and recall.

Making a house: This type of catching teacher in a mistake is very effective when teaching children how to make something. When teaching something to be made, all children must be in a position to see and hear easily. A finished product is shown for them to understand what they will be trying to make. The materials needed are shown to prevent

any interruption in following the steps for working. For an uncomplicated early project, it could be an easy way to make a house. A
rectangular piece of paper, scissors, and paste are all that are necessary.
Explain what folding in half means. Tell how you will try to get the
edges together evenly, then demonstrate. Tell them you will hold the
folded side while you cut off a corner on the open side—demonstrate
this as well. When you open the paper they can see the house shape with
a roof. This always seems to surprise some, so go through the steps
again. It does not matter whether the corner cut off is a big one or a small
one. Then show how one of the corner pieces can be cut to make a
chimney, and how to use just a little paste on a finger tip to spread
smoothly without having lumps of paste.

When all the proper steps have been explained, tell the group you
are going to pretend you are just learning how to make a house and they
must help you. Hold up the paper and start to fold it crookedly. Have
someone tell you the proper way. Then hold the open edge side, making
sure they see what you do. Have someone tell what you said about the
side to hold. When it is time to cut, make it look as though your scissors
would cut a straight line and say, "Now I'll cut straight up (or across)
here." They must tell the direction you should go. Continue each step
with errors—holding scissors a poor way, putting a big lump of paste
on, etc. This includes visual training as well as listening. They go
hand-in-hand.

Developing Listening Skills

Hearing sounds: There are many activities to enhance listening
skills, and they are fun to do for short group periods. By having them
readily available, aides could use them for individual help. Show a set of
objects such as wood, tin, glass, and plastic. Let the children see you tap
them and hear the different sounds they make. Then have one child turn
away. He tries to tell what is tapped while he is not looking. This can
later be more exacting by selecting articles more closely related such as a
solid block, a hollow block, and a cardboard box; a musical bell, a
triangle, and a long nail on a string; a can, a plastic glass, and a glass jar.

Piano tones: For a group activity, the children watch as you play
low notes on the piano, then the middle and high notes. Repeat the
contrast between low and high notes. The group then turns away from

the piano. When high notes are sounded, the children stretch up; they stoop down for low notes and just stand for middle notes.

Using the piano, vibrations can be explained. Most of the children will grasp the idea of invisible sound waves that bring sounds to their ears. They all enjoy feeling the vibrations and begin to understand the concept of sound waves after they have had the physical experience.

The panel on the front of the piano can be removed for viewing the harp strings as the hammers strike them. This new experience can be an exciting one for children. They can hear how the vibrations are stopped when the string is touched. You should locate which harp string sounds for a specific low key, as the vibrations on the large strings are more easily felt. Let each child come to have his fingers placed gently on the harp string while the note is being struck. They can be asked, "Do you feel the vibrations?" to have the principle of sound and its name become associated. This same science principle can be demonstrated by using a triangle. Ring it while holding it properly. Then try to ring it while holding the metal. Let children tell what they remember about vibrations.

Classifying sounds: When children are learning to hear high or low sounds, they can also listen for voice tones that convey emotions. Say some simple phrase such as, "I see it" to show joy, sadness, surprise, and fear. Let them try to express an emotion you suggest. Talk about and classify loud noises, soft noises, happy sounds, and sad sounds. You could have charts for the sounds that might show pictures or printed words. Indoors or outside, there should be some time allotted to just listen for the sounds around them. Too often we don't really listen to the birds; sounds become noises that may be shut out unless they are very loud.

The piano and phonograph music can train listening. There can be listening for a particular instrument, for fast or slow music, and for loud or soft sounds. They can try to keep time to the music. If you play the piano, you give some good listening training by abruptly changing the piece you are playing. Go from a skipping tune to walking, running, or tip-toe music. Do not warn when the change will come and those who merely follow the lead of others will be easily spotted.

Matching sounds: For individual activities, collect a set of jars or bottles that cannot be seen through and put rice, sand, beans, or pebbles in them. The object is to match the pairs by shaking them. The same idea can be used by putting in different amounts of one material in matching bottles. There might be just one bean in each of two bottles, two in two others, six in another pair and quite a few more in a fourth set. This takes careful listening. The same type of activity can be used by putting water in bottles, having two with the same amount of water so each pair gives the same tone when tapped. After seeing them as they are tapped (to gain an understanding of what is being done) have a child, with eyes covered, try to tap the bottles and match a pair.

DEVELOPING GOOD SEQUENTIAL MEMORY SKILLS

Hearing sounds and identifying them is preliminary to remembering what is heard. Of course you do not use one week or month to listen for sounds and another to use recall. They dovetail although the concentration may be more in one area than another. As you are training for intelligent listening, memory becomes a concomitant skill. When listening is purposeful and a need to listen is felt, recall can be developed. It can be as ordinary as the need to remember a set of directions in order to be able to go on to a further desired action. ("After you have put away the things on your table, be sure the paste is back in the jar, all scraps are picked up, and your aprons put away. Then you may come for a game.") Any part of the directions forgotten means delay and going back to complete them.

Not just memory, but the ability to recall in sequential order is of vital importance. There must be good listening skills to learn to attend to the order of what was heard. Early in the year, the attention span is rather short and the listening habits for some may be poor, indicating that the early patterns of directions should be short. Probably two directions in order will be all some can remember at a time. The first things to be made that are explained will be quite uncomplicated. The directions for procedure will be given a step at a time. There is no set time to wait to increase the number of directions that can be handled comfortably as a group, and individuals in the group vary in ability. When children learn to listen with a purpose and interest the ability to cope with more directions comes more quickly.

In many cases there will be children having a need for individual training. The teacher might use a few minutes, during some activity period while the others are occupied, to go through one of the following exercises with one child. It would be more satisfactory to have an aide take the child for training at a regularly specified time. What these children receiving individual help miss by not doing what the rest of the group may be doing is more than compensated for when they are gaining the necessary skills for easy learning. If there is a project that is desirable for all to do, and it is interrupted so an individual can have a special time for some training, an aide or mother-helper in the room could go over the steps in directions with the child when he returns a short time later.

Sequential Memory Exercises
to Be Used With Individuals

Series of numbers: After hearing a short series of numbers such as 1-6-3, the child repeats them in order. Then change the order and also use other series of numbers. The series are kept short to insure success. The child should receive some word of praise for each correct response. The length of the sequence is increased by one number when several of the various shorter series are quickly and correctly repeated. Colors or letters of the alphabet could be used in the same manner for a change in routine.

Arranging objects: An individual may profit by having practice in following a set of directions. Arrange a variety of objects. Begin with simple directions, such as: "Put the paper under the book, then put the pencil on top of the book." If not done in that order, put the objects back and say, "Listen again." Then repeat the same directions. When the child has successfully handled, in order, a variety of short directions, add a third object.

Rhythmic patterns: Repeating a rhythmic pattern of sounds is used individually or in groups. The teacher claps rather slowly a few claps. The children repeat the same number of claps. Change the number of claps. When the proper number of claps can be repeated readily, use a pattern of claps. It may be one long clap, two quick claps, and then a long clap. Vary the rhythmic patterns. As skill increases, make the patterns a little more complex.

Physical patterns: Physical action directions could be used as a relaxer after a concentrated activity. "Put your hands on your head, then your knees, and then your ankles." "Jump up, stoop down, turn around." Add movements as the sequential skill is easily done.

The child having difficulty must experience success and have it immediately recognized. Do not wait until the end of a session, but give some praise for each successful occurrence. The more his confidence and self-image are improved, the easier it is to advance. He may have a need for encouragement when he is struggling to recall by being told, "You are getting it." For the individual child the training session should not be longer than ten minutes. Do not permit fatigue to set in. If an aide is conducting the session, she should understand the plans to follow. The aide should record and report to the teacher the progress or any difficulties.

Using food as a reward for the children having the greatest difficulty has been successful to many. The food used is often a few bits of a dry cereal, or one piece of M and M candy. It is given at the end of a session when a child has at least put forth effort. It apparently does not disturb the other children not needing the special attention if they happen to see it. Children are quite flexible and understanding. As long as they are receiving their satisfactions of praise for the work they do, the little rewards for others are easily ignored.

Sequential Memory Exercises for a Group

I went to the store: One group sequential memory game is the old one of "I went to the store and bought——." The first person says one thing he bought. The next one repeats what the first one said and adds one more item. Each one must repeat what went before and then tell one more thing he bought. If someone can't remember, the next child may try. According to the ability of the group, and to keep it from becoming too difficult, there should be a place to stop the series and have a fresh start.

Repeating a story: Tell a short story to be retold. Tell the children to listen carefully as you hope it can be repeated the way it was heard. The story should be only a few sentences; something simple and ordinary can be made up. "I went for a walk. I saw some flowers. Then I saw birds fly into a tree. Next, I heard a boat whistle." It should be retold in sequence. More than one may try. No criticism or impatience is shown for efforts that fail. There can be time for children to retell some story they have heard. This should be a story they all know so recall can be checked. If the one telling the story forgets what happened next, another may continue as far as he is able. These story telling attempts should be kept in a light fun mood. The teacher's constant pleasure for their succeeding as far as possible must be evident. When one bogs down, it wasn't failure, but just going as far as possible at the moment.

Recalling objects: There are visual recall methods using objects seen and then removing one to recall the one missing. The same type of activity can be done orally. Say a series of three numbers, colors, or shapes. Then omit one during a repetition. Have the children tell which item is missing. Then go to four items. Or say, "I want a red, a yellow, and a green piece of paper." Then show papers of several colors and have someone pick out the pieces you want. They should get them in the proper order.

A more complicated set of directions for more advanced listening could be, "I am going to make a design. I will need one long piece of paper, two square pieces, and three round pieces." Someone selects the proper pieces in order. Or you could say the pieces needed and then show the pieces in the same sequence, but leaving out one set. Have them tell which is missing.

The same type of activity can be used with numbers or other objects by naming them and then showing a set with one missing. Vary this by naming a series of articles. A child then puts the articles named in the proper order.

Acting a story: For sequential memory with action you could tell a short story for someone to act out in order. "I was going to the playground. First I walked, then I ran, and then I hopped. I stopped to rest and then walked to the playground." Some children may still need a story with only a few actions so they can feel success too. A story may be "Bobby took a trip. First he went in a car. Then he rode on a train. Next, he rode in a boat. He came back on a plane. Now find the pictures and put them up in the order Bobby rode on them."

Older students in the school could handle the individual auditory training necessary for some kindergarteners after they are told just how to proceed. A responsible older child puts forth sincere effort, and the younger child responds well to him. This also has proved to be a great opportunity for an older student, not able to achieve status in other ways, to become important by being an aide.

ACTIVITIES TO DEVELOP THE ABILITY
FOR HEARING RHYMING SOUNDS

As auditory perception becomes more acute, rhyming words can be recognized. The teacher may introduce them as words that sound alike. For most kindergarten children, rhyming word perception is fairly easy. After explaining what is meant by the term "rhyming words," the teacher says some series of them—cat, rat, fat, hat, sat, mat, pat, bat; pan, ran, can, man, tan, fan, van—saying them carefully, and enunciating clearly. Then the teacher may say a word and have the response be a rhyming word. It could be fun for a child to try to say a word that rhymes with his name. This is more satisfactory than having another child do it as other children often try to say some silly word that may embarrass the child.

CONCLUSION

It is very obvious that good auditory perception is of paramount importance if much learning is to take place. All the fundamentals of learning have listening processes. To insure intelligent listening, not only must the words be understood, but they must be retained. Not only must they be retained, but the order in which they were heard must be recalled, or the attempted learnings could be confused and the end result changed.

If the habit of attention is not acquired early, the need to listen and understand what is presented may become so delayed it will become very difficult to overcome lost ground. There is evidence today that sequential listening has long been neglected. Many children showing learning problems get positive assistance when they are taken through the steps of recalling auditory sequential patterns. It helps prepare for the learnings necessary as more structured instruction takes place. The ability to listen and process the information is essential at all stages of learning. There must first be assurance there is no physical impairment to hinder hearing. Then the background of each child must be known to establish a level of communication. When any possible obstructions are cleared, the atmosphere and attitudes for intelligent listening for satisfactory understanding must be established.

DEVELOPING REASONING
WITH LEARNING

6

It is extremely important to include training in reasoning with the development of a child's perceptual skills. It will affect the child's thinking in regard to what is perceived, the association of the perceptions with known facts or experiences, and the anticipation of continuing events. It will affect a choice of the most advantageous and appropriate reactions or responses by the child.

Reasoning about an object may concern decisions about its relation to other objects, the way it is best used or placed, and whether its size, shape, or directionality identifies it as a desired choice. Auditory perceptions must form associations in a child's mind which will allow him to continue a thought to its logical conclusion, and to derive implied meanings.

Individualized activities in this chapter that would aid slower children are: any of the creative art activities, "Balancing," "What is needed," all uses of pictures, particularly categorizing (using more obvious ones), "Matching pairs," "Completing sentences," "Ending a story," "Knock-knock," and "Descriptive words."

Brighter children can also benefit from the art creations, "Balancing," "What is it," "Objects with pictures," all uses of pictures that draw more detailed observation and more comprehensive responses,

"Where do they belong," "How are they alike," "Guess my picture," "Nonsense words," "Mix-ups," "Ending a story," "What would happen if," "Why are they made this way," and "Descriptive words."

COMING TO LOGICAL CONCLUSIONS

The richness of background experiences, including a good concept of words, furnishes a child with degrees of mental resource material that can facilitate reasoning. The child who is fortunate enough to have learned about nature, perhaps in his own yard or community, and to have shared with others a variety of stimulating activities, has a great advantage over those with few such opportunities. Past experiences and known facts must be recalled to facilitate logical decisions.

Some children with well meaning older brothers and sisters have had everything done for them. They have had everything explained and answers given before there were questions. These overly-assisted children come to school unable, at times, to solve the most elementary tasks. Many have no idea of how to proceed when faced with the need to put on wearing apparel. Some put their coats on upside down. During an activity period, they appear to have a difficult time making choices or decisions about what they will use. They have had neither cause, nor opportunity, to solve the simplest tasks. Such children need much understanding and encouragement to become independent thinkers. They have a need for some individual help to overcome their long established habit of merely accepting any and all decisions made by others.

Individual help may be given to these children in different situations. When putting on outer wearing apparel, they can decide whether to put on their overshoes or leggings first. While using blocks, the child could be asked to select the most suitable ones to fit a designated space. When using a simple puzzle, he can try to decide on a missing piece before trying to place it, and tell why he made the decision. He will probably have an initial need for leading suggestions to notice colors, lines, and shapes when he is learning to have reasons for his selections.

These children can profit by having aides give individual help. They must initially be encouraged to decide everything possible that concerns them in the classroom. Their attempts to make decisions should be praised by the teacher. Accomplishing a task may take a longer time for them than for others while they are acquiring the habits of decision making and problem solving.

In all aspects and activities of a classroom, there is some degree of reasoning and coming to conclusions by the child. Children may decide who sits in the front and who sits in the back to enable everyone to see clearly when a movie is shown. Deciding whether it is better to use cymbals or a triangle during a particular passage of music requires reasoning. A child should be encouraged to plan the location for performing his particular activity. He should be guided into considering the space, the access to materials that may be needed, possible conflicts with work other children are doing, and general traffic patterns.

When behavioral patterns are being established, and points may be earned, children must decide on the behavior that will earn the results that are desired. Coming to these logical conclusions becomes a reflexive action in many behavioral situations. When the children become conditioned to the satisfaction of receiving positive reinforcement for their decisions of acceptable behavior, they no longer have to think, "If I do this, (something) will result." However, the past experience must be recalled initially to arrive at satisfactory conclusions.

Children using blocks should be expected to plan the appropriate placement of the blocks to insure stability in any construction. They should decide on the sizes of blocks that are best suited for the project that is planned. The block builders can be expected to construct a project that is identifiable to other children. Other children should be able to tell what the building is, and why they think so. As a further activity in reasoning and logic, when the building is taken down, the children should observe the placement of the blocks to decide which ones should be removed first to avoid crashing blocks.

Children planning a creative project that makes use of paper should learn to select the sizes of paper that are best suited for the work. They should be encouraged to reason and decide about the appropriateness of the materials, such as size, color, and their conservation. Small pieces needed for a project could come from the scrap box.

Coming to logical conclusions is an obvious byproduct of solving problems involving numbers. The teacher should arrange many number problems for reasoning such as:

"There are five children who are to sit at the table. There are three chairs. What will you do so that each child will have a chair?"

"Four children were coming to a party. There were six glasses on the table. What will you do to have just enough glasses on the table for each child to have one?"

Children must have an understanding of comparative terms if some reasoning problems are to be solved. A good vocabulary, as well as a good concept of words, is essential for reasoning.

"John has three pencils. Bill has one less than John. How many pencils does Bill have?"

"There are three piles of rocks. One pile has very large rocks, one pile has middle-sized rocks, and one is a pile of small rocks. If you want to fill a box, and use the fewest rocks, from which pile will you take the rocks? If you wanted to have the most rocks in your box, which pile would you choose?"

Listening to stories involves reasoning when there is active participation by the children. There is anticipation as to what will happen next. In addition, when children tell their own stories, they must be involved with sequential ordering reasoning to have the story end logically.

Reasoning is involved with auditory discrimination when the context of a sentence can help the decision of which letter sound should be used or was heard, ă, ĭ, or ŏ, if the sentence is, "He hit the ball."

Logical conclusions are necessary to decide the best site for playing an active game, or the game that can be played with the equipment that is available.

GAMES AND ACTIVITIES TO DEVELOP VISUAL REASONING

It is important to use judgment with accurate visual perception if profitable actions, or reactions, are to result. Children must be taught to actively participate in forming judgments, rather than to passively wait for directions.

Using Reasoning to Create Pictures

Making a house: Early in the year, while homes are being discussed, have colored paper that is pre-cut into suitable sizes for the parts of houses. Have larger pieces for the body of the house, squares and rectangles for the doors, windows, and chimneys. Showing the different sizes and colors, have the children decide what the pieces should be. After you have cut the shape of a roof from a larger piece, hold up a shape that is to be a window. Place it on the roof and ask if that would be an appropriate place for a window. Hold it on other places and have the children tell why, or why not, it is a place for a window. Follow the same procedure with the door and chimney. Ask different children to respond in order to permit the less aggressive ones an opportunity to voice an opinion. After the children understand the way to organize and plan their work, they can work independently.

Make a person: Having assorted sizes of circles and rectangles, tell the children they will make a "fun" sort of person. Using a flannel board, have the children tell which pieces you should pin up to be used to form the parts of the body. Ask why that shape or size was selected. The children can then select the pieces they want and create their own person.

Geometric shapes: Put out sets of shapes in different sizes: round, square, rectangle, and triangle. Ask for ideas as to what specific things could be created when using all of the shapes. Have some of the suggestions quickly pinned up. Suggest something to make and have the children take turns adding a piece at a time while the group watches and agrees or disagrees. If they disagree, the child having a turn may explain his choice and possibly convince the others.

Remove the set of round shapes and ask if the same things could be made. Remove the squares and see if the triangles or rectangles can be arranged as substitutes. Let them arrange their own pictures.

Torn paper: Prepare quantities of torn paper scraps in many sizes. Pin a few of them to the flannel board, and then ask for any ideas as to what you might be making. Pin up a few more, and ask if the ideas have changed, and why. You could tell them you have now decided it should become a tree, a dog, a garden, or whatever, and ask different ones to tell what pieces could be left, taken away, or added to become the new idea. Then have the children each decide on a specific thing to make. They should later identify their pictures.

Wiggly line pictures: Have each child draw a wiggly line—a form of an "s," a curved line with a loop, a wavy line—any place on a piece of paper. They then trade their papers with another child. Using a different color, they try to add lines to make some recognizable object or picture. They can have fun showing and identifying their pictures.

Block Activities

Balancing: Bring out different sizes of blocks. Ask which blocks should go on the top and the bottom to build a tower. Why? Have a long board to be balanced on one block. Ask where the block should be placed under the board for it to balance. Have blocks of other sizes ready. When the board is balanced, ask a child to choose two blocks that he and another child could place on the opposite ends of the board at the same time and keep the board in balance. Could someone figure a way to place two blocks at one end, and one block at the other end, and still have the board balance? They may decide to use two small blocks and one large one, to change the distances from the ends of the board, or someone may reason a need for a different placement of the supporting block.

Objects Used for Reasoning

Who has it?: This game is a good mental exercise for both memory and reasoning. Choose four different small objects that can each be held, unseen, in a closed hand. The children sit in a circle with their closed hands in their laps. After the four objects are identified and observed by the group, one child passes them out, one at a time, to any four children. He then must go back and ask, "May I have the ———?" It is not necessary to get them in order. If the child he asks does not have the particular object asked for, or possibly nothing at all, he only answers, "I do not have the ———." He does not open his hands to show whether or not he has an item. Some children forget the articles they have passed, some forget which children received an object. Alert children will recall each child having an object. If they have collected one or two things and can recall a child having something, but not what it is, by looking at what has been gotten back they can figure what is left to collect. The reasoning thinkers will ask the child for one item after another until he gets the right one, instead of going from one child to another and asking for one thing at a time. Reasoning is also demonstrated when a child, observing others, realizes possible difficulties and decides on a method of passing out and collecting the objects. He may decide to give the objects to four children sitting by each other, and then to collect them in reverse order. The game is not as easy as it appears to be at first. The challenge is enjoyed, and the game gets many requests to have it played again. If a child is having difficulties even recalling who has the articles, he could then get the assistance of having those children identify themselves. He is apt to be able to get at least some of the things. This is to avoid the feeling of failure. Praise him for what he does get.

What is needed?: In the center of the circle, put out various items that could be used in different activities. Do not have them grouped in categories. They could be things used when playing (dolls, balls, toys), when building (hammer, saw, nails, wood), sewing needs (scissors, thread, needles, cloth), things to make pictures (paper, paint brush, crayons, pencil), ways to travel (car, train, plane, boat). Then ask someone to select the articles that might be needed for the activity you specify. Some of the items may be used for more than one activity.

What is it?: Place several objects, or pictures of objects, in the center of the children's circle. Describe one of the items. Have one child at a time try to guess what it is. He should ask in a sentence, "Is it the ____?" The descriptions may concern the size, shape, color, the materials of which it is made, its parts or use, or in the way it may move. There should be a reason for choosing one item rather than another. You may have a red car and a red dump truck. The description could be, "It is made of metal, it is red, it has four wheels, people often use it on the highways when they are taking a vacation." You could include a blue ball, and a blue wooden block, a tent, a house, a cabin, and the like.

Objects with pictures: The use of objects adds interest with the observation of pictures. Have a box of objects that relate in some way to a picture that is shown. The picture would have several subjects in it. A child closes his eyes and draws an object from the box. Then he finds the part of the picture where it would logically belong—a wheel for a car, a nail for a building, a piece of cloth for clothes, a leaf for a tree, and so on.

Pictures to Aid Reasoning

What is happening?: Show a picture to have the children tell what is happening. This does not mean naming the objects pictured. Is it a happy picture or a sad one? Why? Is it a noisy or a quiet picture, and why? Children may have different opinions, but they should give their reasons. They also may be able to decide what they think could be being said by any people pictured.

What comes next?: Fold a picture and show one side of it. Have turns to tell what could be pictured on the other side. A picture of a child bending over and holding out a hand could suggest several logical things to be expected in the rest of the picture. A face showing an expression of surprise or happiness could elicit a variety of things that might be expected to be seen.

Sequential order: Have different series of pictures that belong in some sequential order. One series could include a tree with bare branches, the tree with green leaves, the tree with blossoms, the tree with fruit, and the tree with a few brown leaves. Another series might be one of pictures illustrating a well-known story or rhyme. Display them out of order. Have children arrange them in their proper order.

Which one?: Show a group of pictures and then describe one. A child selects the picture by the description. For children having difficulty, the descriptions may be of the obvious features. A more advanced step could be to include in the description an object or action that only one picture shows, such as a boat moving and one docked. Children who are able to reason well could have more subtle descriptions such as find the picture that shows happiness; find the picture that lets us know someone is going to take a trip.

What happens?: Using pictures showing such things as a picnic basket, a suitcase, fishing gear, balls and bats, pails and shovels, a car, a car with luggage, and the like, have a child select a picture and tell what he thinks could happen next. There could be many different logical answers.

Tell a story: Have three of four pictures that could relate in some way and suggest a continuity of action. They might be of a child alone, a pet alone, a child and a pet together; a city or country scene, people with suitcases, ways to travel, a family at home. Show a set that is in any order. Have a child arrange them in his chosen way and tell his story according to his order of the pictures.

Reasoning by Categorizing Pictures

Find them: Using an assortment of pictures the tasks could be:

- Find the things that move about in the air.
- Find the things that do not have fur.
- Find the things you can (cannot) eat.
- Find what you use when it is cold.
- Find the things that are not alive. (In this series, include plants or trees to check their understanding of the word "alive.")

The directions can become more specific, such as:

- Find the things that are alive that you could have at your home.
- Find the things you can eat that grow on trees.
- Find the places that are safe for playing a game of ball.

Match pairs: Some pictures can be matched logically in pairs. You might have a bird and a nest, a horse and a barn, a car and a garage, a child and a house, and so on. They might be objects that are used together—hammer and nails, thread and needle, pencil and paper, glasses and eyes. Some children may be ready for less obvious differences. You might have pictures of wood and a house, cloth and a dress, seeds and plants, and a stove and a cooked meal. Arrange the pictures out of order. Children take turns to match two of the pictures. When working with a group of varied abilities, include pictures that are easier to match and offer the first opportunities to the less able children.

Where do they belong?: Select pictures of many types of buildings. The task could be to sort the buildings as to the ones you could find on a farm, in a city, buildings where people shop, or where they might live. Reasons should be given for the selections.

Another selection could be of animals to group according to pets, zoo animals, or farm animals.

Collect pictures of a bedroom, a living room, an outdoor scene, a snowy picture, a pool, etc. Have other pictures of different types of clothing and have children select the things that should be worn with each of the first pictures.

With almost any assortment of pictures, you can plan questions that require reasoning to answer them. When the pictures are in labeled folders, they are ready for immediate use by aides or the teacher.

DEVELOPING AUDITORY REASONING

Good auditory perception, retention, and reasoning go together. As stated in the chapter on auditory skills, tones and inflections of the voice create an understanding of emotions. Reasoning interprets the sounds heard to indicate an anticipation of something happy, or not so happy, as being meant. Children can hear sounds and then can reason what might be happening whether it is a crashing noise, a siren, or a car's horn. Little pattering sounds might cause an expectation of rain, but reasoning eliminates the possibility of large objects falling. Provide listening times to hear sounds that happen out of the room, and let the children decide what could be happening.

Activities and Games Requiring Reasoning

How are they alike?: Playing the game of "How are they alike?" encourages intense thinking. It is a good idea to have a list of questions prepared. "How are people and clocks alike?" (They both have hands and faces.) "How is a chair like a dog?" (They both have four legs and a back.) "How is a piano like a car?" (They both must have keys.) "How is a goat like a car?" (They both have horns.) "How is an egg like a turtle?" (They both have shells.) An easy introduction to the game might be, "How are birds and airplanes alike?"

Guess my picture: Give some children pictures of some individual objects that are commonly known. A child with a picture gives one or two clues about his picture: "It is something to eat. It is sweet." "It has a shell and it lives in the water." "It can cut." "It has fur and a long, thin, tail." "It is very big and has a short tail." The teacher may prefer to give the clues. Children take turns to guess, and try to see which one can collect the most pictures by their correct guesses.

Completing sentences: Begin a sentence and have a child complete it in his own way. More than one completion will be correct. "A tree fell down when ____." "There was a big puddle of water in our yard because ____." "We waded in the ____." "We went for a ride to ____, and we rode there on (in) ____." "The loud noise we heard was ____." "You could tell the people were happy because ____." "Some things move slowly. Slowly as a ____."

Nonsense words: Using sentences from books, select some having easily understood words. Read a sentence and, in it, substitute a nonsense word. "Johnny could make the ball go far when he hit it with his *bling.*" Children try to get the proper word by the context of the sentence.

Mix-ups: Caution the children that they must listen carefully to a short story, as it will be all mixed up, and they must try to get it in the order it must have happened. Tell them to keep count of the number of things that happen. Tell the story slowly and repeat it.

"Henry went into the house, left the playground, went to bed, put on his pajamas, ate his supper."

"Davey put on his coat, woke up, ate breakfast, got dressed, got out of bed."

Maintain the spirit of fun with each attempt. If the different actions are forgotten after a few tries, ask them to listen again while you repeat the story. This activity develops memory, auditory, and reasoning skills.

Ending a story: Read a part of a story that is new to the group. Before you come to the end of the story, have some children tell what they think the ending might be. Then finish the story for them to see how their stories compare with the author's ending. At other times, pause during a story where there is anticipation, and ask what they think is going to happen next.

ACTIVITIES FOR ABSTRACT REASONING

Reasoning in the abstract takes place in many activities. Planning daily work may require it. "What will be needed for the work you plan to do?" "The building does not seem to be strong. What can be used to improve it?"

When using science equipment abstract thinking will be required to answer why, what, or where questions. Experiments, given in the chapter on science, are demonstrated for the children, but the causes for the reactions are left for children to solve. When children realize there are answers to the things that puzzle them, and with effort they can be solved, they are more apt to try to discover the solution by themselves.

When the principle is understood, it becomes possible to extend some experiments the way one 5-year-old boy did. After experimenting with the repelling and attracting forces of magnets, he wanted to use the force to move a car. He built a car using plastic Rig-A-Jig pieces. When he tried the magnets, the one on the car just slid forward when the second magnet was near. He was reminded to think about what magnets would cling to. There were flat pieces of metal available. With the remark, "O.K., now just let me figure this out," he created a little car he could cause to not only go forward, but to turn. This demonstration was a tremendous boost for the efforts of the others.

There will be abstract reasoning when children understand numbers and mathematical terms. They learn to draw conclusions about quantities observed. If they are shown four squares with two shapes in one, three in another, eight and ten in the others, and are then asked to find the one with ten shapes, with good reasoning some will begin counting the last two immediately.

What would happen if?: Have the children imagine some extreme situations that are asked.

What would happen if:
The school did not have a roof?
There was no more water in the world?
Birds did not have feathers?
All the trees were gone?
All the ground was covered with cement?
All the rocks were sponges?
It did not ever rain?

Knock-knock: Play a guessing game using things that can be located in the room when you say to a child, "Knock, knock, I have four legs and a flat top. What am I?" "Knock, knock, I have six sides. You can lift one of my sides and put things into me. What am I?" "Knock, knock. I have a back and legs but I cannot walk. What am I?" "Knock, knock. I have two hands and a face. I stay in one place and people look at me once in a while." "Knock, knock. I can be very bright, but I do not know anything. What am I?" "Knock, knock. I have many keys, but I cannot open anything. What am I?" "Knock, knock. I have many leaves, but I do not grow. What am I?"

Why are they made this way?: Have pairs of pictures of related things that have different uses and will require reasoning to explain the need for the differences. With pictures of big, heavy truck or airplane tires, and small tires for a car, ask why they must be so different. Why must a truck use the big tires that cause it to be so much higher than a car?

Have pictures of buildings. If you ask why some buildings are taller than they are wide, be sure the terms are understood. Show a picture of a fenced playground and an open field. Ask why the fence is put in one place and not the other. Pictures showing a ramp leading into a storage or loading dock, and steps by another building or a house can create reasoning as to why they are made that way. You may have to lead their reasoning if there are some answers, such as, "That is the way they were made." Or, "Somebody wanted them that way." To stimulate thinking, get them to think how they are used or how much space is there to be used.

Descriptive words: Tell the children you will say some words and they are to tell what they might describe and why. There will be many possible answers: fast-slow-tall-short-heavy-loud-soft-quiet-small-big. After the children have made their choices for "big" and "small," read, *Let's Find Out What's Big and What's Small,* by Charles and Martha Shapp, Franklin Watts, Inc. Then see if there are different decisions some may want to make. Will that change their decisions for some of the other words?

Reminders to be sure of the understanding or word meanings have been repeated with good cause. It can be the difference between success and a feeling of failure. After explaining rhyming words are words that sound alike, and the group was responding easily, one boy would be apt to say "boy," or "father" when he heard "man." Taking him alone, the rhyming sets of words were slowly, and carefully repeated for him. He said, "You are just saying words that sound the *same*." It was the word "alike" that confused him and his need for individualized instruction was holding him back. Many children respond on a one-to-one basis when they do not appear to function initially in a group.

Another time, while learning to discriminate between sizes, a girl was evidencing difficulty when asked to find the smallest shape. The shapes were very different as to size. The word "smallest" was changed to "the little one," and then, "the tiny one." Realizing she was a greatly protected child, she was asked to find the "baby" one. She selected the proper size immediately. Then she could be taught *to* that need.

Keep the children figuring their own answers when possible. Supply the necessary data, and encourage them to come to logical conclusions through reasoning. When some do not appear to respond in a group situation, provide opportunities for them to have the activities individually. If the materials are ready, any two or three minute break, a waiting time for children to gather, or a pause in a chosen activity can afford the teacher a time for individualized help that is more valuable for the child than having him sit passively for ten minutes in the group situation. When the group is doing the activity, an aide can take one or two children with similar material for individual help.

LEARNING NUMBERS FOR WORK AND FUN

7

Using numbers should be enjoyable, and should give as much satisfaction as creative projects do. When children are presented material that is for their level of ability, they will feel pleasure by being able to cope and learn new facts.

In the average kindergarten class, most of the children come with some rudiments of counting and recognizing numbers. There may be some who cannot count to ten and cannot recognize any numeral. At the other extreme, a few will have the ability to solve some abstract problems and have a good concept of the words that are used in mathematical figuring.

To meet these individual needs, there must be a continuing exposure to the daily seeing and use of numbers. There must be approaches that satisfy individual abilities, from low to high. Each individual must feel he is making progress in learning to read and use numbers.

A variety of activities and games are needed to afford individual progress and the essential feeling of success. Children can learn the use of the signs and symbols that express a mathematical process while they are learning the sequential order of the numbers.

The activities in this chapter best suited for individualized instruction with slower children are: ''Block building,'' ''Store,'' ''Rhymes,''

"Kinesthetic materials," "Chart," "Getting supplies," "Clapping and counting," "Adding," "Matching numerals with sets," "Set adding and subtracting" (according to needs), "Designs and drawings," "Bead cards," "Secret message," "Follow the dots," "Fill in the missing number," "Sample pages," and "Vocabulary."

For more advanced students: writing and figuring attendance figures, "Measuring," "Adding" (using numerals), "Fishing," "Set adding and subtracting," "Rocket to the moon," "Recognizing number combinations," "Follow the dots," "Fill in the missing number," "Sample pages," and "Fractional parts."

EVERYDAY USES FOR NUMBERS

Seeing numerals and using numbers and mathematical terms should be common practices. The need for and the use of numbers will be introduced on the first day by calling attention to the calendar, and a list of September birthday names with their dates can be introduced. There should be a place where the first numerals they will be learning to use and write are mounted, beginning with zero. Shapes, corresponding to the count, should be by each numeral. Kinesthetic numerals, available to use as a chosen activity, are valuable aids. Show the children that the use of numbers or counting happens incidentally many times in a day: Counting the children who are present or absent, counting or measuring materials, reading numbered places, or counting for a game, song, or rhyme contribute to the use of arithmetic.

Using Counting and Recognizing Numerals

Counting the group: When the children have picked up their name cards and have formed a group, say the number of children that belong in the room and write it. Count the ones present, having the children help you count. Write this sum. Show any name cards that may be left. Count the cards and show how they complete the total count. To vary the counting procedure, count the girls and boys separately, writing the numbers. Ask which group has more and which has less. Another variation is to have the girls stand, and have a boy count them. Each girl sits as she is counted. Then have the boys stand and have a girl do the counting. At first you can write the totals. As skills develop, have a child write the totals. If they are written with two numerals, draw attention to the need for the proper placement of the numerals. Guide the children to figure the difference between the totals.

To have the entire group participate in the counting, have the group stand to count off. A child says his number and then sits down. If the children sit in fairly regular locations, begin the counting at different places. The total number belonging and the total number present can be written. Have the children figure the number that are absent, giving more capable children an opportunity to work at their level.

When using name cards for attendance, count the cards that have been left. Count the girls' cards and the boys' cards. Which is more? Put them together while holding them in sets. ''Two boys and one girl make how many that are absent?'' Separate the cards of the children who are absent to show the ways they can be divided to make the same total. With four cards, show them as two and two, three and one, one and three, four ones, and four and zero. Show them to have the children notice the statements as reading from left to right.

Using the calendar: Each day check the calendar. Ask which numeral should be added for the present date. Children can learn to respond with the day, month, and ordinal number. For those having difficulties saying the complete sentence, guide them as to the correct information. Then say the sentence correctly for them while you point to the appropriate places on the calendar. Have them repeat what you said.

Note the time that may elapse until a special day in the month occurs. It might be a holiday, a birthday, or a special school event. Have the children count it as to days or weeks. Call attention to the number of days in one week and the way the weeks can be counted on a calendar. When they are anticipating a special event, remind them, ''Yesterday we had ten days to wait. How many days will it be today?''

Block activities: Block building, when it is purposeful, requires much use of mathematical terms and counting. Blocks must be counted or measured to make the sides of buildings even. Lengths of boards must be compared to fit some pieces. Sizes of blocks must be determined for weight and balance. Children should be guided into these decisions rather than be permitted to make random choices. When they learn to rationalize before selecting materials, children's efforts will be more productive.

Store: A grocery store, a toy shop, a greeting card store, or others may be set up at different times. The differences in the value of coins should be discussed with the group by showing real money to encourage the proper use of play money. Explain why a nickel or a dime is called five cents or ten cents. A cash register and scales add further use of numbers. Their use, and the need to know what is more or less, should be explained.

Counting rhymes: Children having difficulty counting to ten can be aided by counting rhymes.
   1, 2, 3, 4, 5—I caught a hare alive.
   6, 7, 8, 9, 10—I let him go again.
   Also the rhyme, "1, 2, Buckle my shoe, etc." is a good one to use.

Kinesthetic materials: For a different lesson, make numbers for children to feel. Numerals can be cut from sandpaper and glued to cards. White glue can be used to outline the shapes of the numerals heavily. Make a double line of the glue, leaving a space between the lines for finger tracing. They might be made on colored tagboard.

   Show how to roll clay into a rope, and how to shape it into numerals. This is also for individual number practice, and helps some children when they are trying to write their numerals.

Chart: Prepare a chart with the numerals from zero through ten, having pictured shapes by them in corresponding numbers. Explain the meaning of zero. Demonstrate this with objects and mathematical statements. The chart can be a place of reference when a child does not recall the numerals or their number count.

   Use the chart when you are introducing the numbers that will be receiving concentration. If you are using the count from zero through three, point to a numeral and ask a child to hold up their number of fingers. Write a few of each of the numerals out of order. Having turns, say, "Show me a three (a zero, etc.)." A child finds it and says, "This is a three." This is a good exercise for children having a need for individual help in the recall of numerals.

   Point to a numeral and have the children trace it in the air. Watch for left to right movement. Your demonstration must be in reverse when you are facing the group. Have turns to write the numerals on a chalk board.

At another time, have the children write the numerals that have been practiced, and draw the same number of balls, apples, pumpkins, or whatever by each numeral.

Getting supplies: When planning a project that requires paper, a child can be expected to consider the sizes of the papers that are needed, as well as the number of pieces. Some projects direct the selection as to the number of pieces to be taken. "To make the witch, take four triangles." When planning some work, the comparative terms will be used. "To make a person, what should the largest circle become? What will a very small circle be?"

Helpers, serving groups of children, must figure the numbers of papers with paste that are needed to have one paper for each two children. When serving at a party, they must count the napkins, dishes, and spoons they may need.

Measuring: The ruler is used to measure and draw lines. The yardstick or ruler can be used to measure pieces of paper for some specific use, or to mark off certain spaces necessary to do a task. The growth of children is measured in inches or feet and inches. The comparative terms are used when children stand back-to-back. Then the tallest one can stand by an aide, or the teacher, to see if "tallest" is still true.

Game turns: Many game turns and parts are decided by number counts.

Swim and Net is a game that goes quickly and furnishes relaxation. Standing in a circle, count off by "one" and "two." All the "ones" take one step forward, and hold hands with their arms raised. They are the net. The "twos" take two steps back to be the fish. At the word "swim," the fish go in and out under the raised arms of the net. At the word "net," the arms come down quickly. Any fish that are inside the circle are caught, and must sit in the center. Count the fish that were caught. Then, at the word "swim," the moving is continued until the word "net" catches others. Count each catch. It may be decided, after a few turns, that a number of fish escaped. Reverse the positions of the "ones" and "twos" to have another turn.

ACTIVITIES TO AID RECALL AND SET CONCEPTS

A kindergarten teacher should know the terms that will be used in the first grade and use them in the kindergarten.

Developing Sequential Number Skills

To be able to add or subtract, a child must know the sequential order of the numbers. Some children have difficulty when asked for one more than four because the words are meaningless to them and they are not thinking at the abstract level. They may be able to count by rote to five, but they do not associate the number words with amounts. These children must have individual practice using the number words with objects, actions, and seeing the numerals. They should have opportunities to count children, chairs, or supplies, to relate the words with their uses. They must have auditory, visual, and kinesthetic experiences combined.

Clapping and counting: Children having difficulties need individualized instruction. They could also be taught in a very small group. Some may have to learn how to count the claps. Have them listen while you clap slowly and count to three. Ask how many claps you made. If they answer, "one, two, three," ask what the last number was. Repeat your claps and ask if you made one clap, two claps, or three claps. Tell them to remember the last number because it tells how many claps were made. Have them clap and say the count. Try different numbers of claps for them to count and then tell the total number. When they can recognize the total number, say a number and have them make the claps. Tell them you are going to clap one more clap than two. They are to listen and tell what is one more than two. Progress through the other numbers. Have the numerals where they can see them during the clapping. Keep each session short—about five minutes.

Adding: The chart with the objects numbered from one to ten shows the progression of adding one more. After the chart has been observed and discussed, use the flannel board with objects and numerals. Place a "one" and one object by it. Ask a child to put up one object plus one more than you did under your object. Have him place the total numeral by it. The next child is to say the number just put up and is to add one more to his row. Continue to ten. Say each problem as a statement when it is completed. The more capable children can try to put up just the numerals as statements.

Subtracting: Use the same procedure as you did for adding, but in reverse order. When it can be done easily, say a number and have a child say the number that is one less. Have children try to put up the statements when you give the problems in random order.

While some of the group will be proceeding at a slower rate to establish the basic learning, others will be ready for more challenging work. The work must be planned to care for individual needs. A few minutes of individualized instruction is more valuable than a longer impersonal group time. Children ready for advanced work are entitled to equal attention for their needs. If you cannot have older students or other aides give individualized instruction, you must plan lessons that provide for responses that are adaptable to different abilities. In many cases the questions and problems can be directed to different levels of ability. At other times, you may want to develop a particular skill with a group at a specific level. Have work prepared that some children could do independently while you work with a group. Suggestions for two levels of addition are given in Figures 7-1 and 7-2. Explain the process and show that the first problem is solved. You may have number games to be used quietly that could be checked quickly at the end of the short session. The work should be purposeful.

Aides should observe a class lesson to see the approaches and repetitions that are necessary. This helps the aide understand that one or two correct responses do not necessarily mean that the process is fully understood by the child.

Matching numerals with sets: Using numeral cards and objects on the floor, or by using the flannel board with flannel pieces, arrange sets of objects to be matched by a numeral. Change the procedure by placing the numerals and have objects placed to match.

As children learn to match sets and numerals, two sets can be arranged. The proper numerals are placed under the sets. Then the total of the sets can be expressed by using the mathematical symbols.

Arrange a set of objects. Separate the pieces to show the different combinations that can add up to the same total.

x	+	x	=	2	1	+	1	= 2
1	+	1	=	2	x	+	x	= 2
xx	+	x	=		2	+	1	=
xxx	+	x	=		3	+	1	=
xxxx	+	x	=		4	+	1	=
xxxxx	+	x	=		5	+	1	=
xxxxxx	+	x	=		6	+	1	=

Figure 7-1

$1 + 3 = 4$	$\times + \times\times\times = 4$
$2 + 3 =$	
$3 + 3 =$	
$4 + 3 =$	
$5 + 3 =$	
$6 + 3 =$	
$7 + 3 =$	

Figure 7-2

Games to Develop Recall and Set Concepts

Sit and say: After the first numerals have been introduced, games can aid their recognition and retention. Numeral cards are scattered on the floor. After a group reading of the numerals, one child turns away while another child sits on a card. He must know the name of the numeral he chose. The first child asks, "Are you sitting on ____?" The other child must answer, "I am (I am not) sitting on ____." When there are several numerals being used, the children must learn to read them in sequential order to be able to decide which one is covered.

Fishing: Prepare two sets of tagboard fish. Each set should have the number of fish that corresponds to the numerals that are to be read. On one set write the numerals. On the other, draw numbers of shapes that correspond to the numerals. The numerals, or shapes, represent the pounds each fish weighs. When marking the shapes on the fish, group them to encourage the recognition of totals by groups. Two red shapes and two green shapes can be read quickly as two and two are four. Put a paper clip at the mouth of each fish. Tie a magnet on a string that is tied to a rod to be a fishing pole.

Each fisherman should have a paper to record his catch. He should write each numeral and make that number of line marks by it. At the end of the game the lines can be counted for a total of the pounds of fish each one caught.

Set adding and subtracting: The children sit in a circle. Scatter large sheets of paper on the floor corresponding to the numbers that are being taught. Have cards with the numerals and a box of blocks at hand. If you are developing set concepts to five, on five pieces of paper have children place blocks, from one to five, on each sheet. Give the cards to a child to have him place them by their proper set of blocks. The group is asked, "Do you agree?"

You then move the cards, placing each one by a different set of blocks. Going by turns, ask a child to find a specific numeral and stand by that set. Ask, "Does that card match the set? How many blocks are in that set? What will you have to do to the set to have it match the card?" The child must answer, "I will add (take away) ____ blocks." He then does it to prove his answer. If a child makes a mistake, let him try it and then correct his own mistake. The group is not to call out answers. When the solution is correct, say the problem as a statement. Give praise for each effort and correct response. When a child corrects his mistake, say, "I knew you could do it." The group, while not correcting errors, can be asked after block changes, "Do you agree?"

To suit individual abilities, the selections can be planned to have the children who are less capable find sets that require the change of only one block. They are still learning the process and can feel that they are successfully competing with the group. The game maintains sufficient interest to continue changing the cards after each set has been corrected, permitting all the children have a turn. The problems can be directed according to individual needs and abilities.

Individual adding and subtracting: Children evidencing difficulties with the group activity can profit by having individual help. An aide can use a flannel board in the same way. The first three or four sets should be used until they can be done easily by the change of one or two objects. The sets and numerical differences should be planned according to skills and needs.

Bus passengers: Arrange ten chairs in two rows to be a bus. Another chair is in front for the driver. A child draws a numeral from a box of cards numbered from one to ten. He announces the number of passengers he will choose according to the number he drew. The bus driver must then decide the number of other passengers he must get to fill the bus. When you know the driver cannot figure abstractly, have the child who drew the card select his passengers and have them sit in the bus. Then have the driver count the empty places. Reinforce the combinations by summarizing when the bus is filled, and show the corresponding numeral cards.

Bunny bounce: The record, RRC 1003, Rhythm Record Company, Oklahoma City, Oklahoma, requires a quick recognition of numerals. Children jump on numbered squares, which are provided, according to direction.

Before or after: Turn numbered cards up, one at a time. The child's response is to be the number that comes either before or after the one on the card. This can be a quick group game for an individual, or it can be used by two children who are adept with sequential counting, to check each other. The children with weak counting ability can be shown low numbers.

Activities for Small Group or Individual Use

Designs and drawings: For a painting project, have the children fold or rule their papers into spaces. Have them select two implements that are to be dipped into paint and pressed onto the paper to make repeat designs. Each shape is to be pressed in a space a specified number of times, alternating the use of the shapes. If they select a spool and a sponge, they might make four impressions of the spool in the first space, three with the sponge in the next space, back to four with the spool in the third space, etc. This requires attention to counting and the order of use. The child sets his pattern.

A seasonal activity is to have the children draw some objects —pumpkins, feathers, trees—in sequentially ordered sets to identify the sets with numerals.

Rocket to the moon: Prepare a large chart with a moon at the top. A strip, extending from the base of the chart to the moon, is numbered from one to one hundred. Print the numbers through twenty. They may become difficult to read above that. The remainder could be done by identifying increases by tens, and using lines between them for the other numbers. Have a small tagboard rocket for each child with his name on it. A child counts as far as he can go, and his rocket is pinned at that level until a later attempt may raise it. This activity can be started with the group watching. It can be continued, a few at a time, as there is time with the group, or it can be done individually during any other activity time when you may be free to hear a counting turn. Children sometimes count fast and forget whether they said the fifties or the sixties. Watching their rocket as it is moved up the numbered strip often helps them to be able to continue their count.

Bead cards: To keep individual records of sequential counting, prepare a chart having the children's names listed on one side. The chart is ruled into squares, heading each vertical row of squares from one to ten. Have cards that are numbered from one to ten, with a slit cut at the top where a child may slip in the end of a bead string. A child selects a card, puts his name on it, and strings beads according to the number on the card. He attaches the string to the card and leaves it in a designated place to be checked and have the chart marked. Children can do this at their own pace.

Secret message: This conceptual game is fun for the group to watch while the writing of numerals is being learned and can be used individually. To have the turns go more quickly, if you have a large blackboard space, have several children face the board at a time. Ask the waiting children to watch the secret message you put on each child to see if the writers get your message. Use only the two or three numbers being worked on at the time, repeating them on different backs. If a child reverses his number, ask him to feel it again. Be sure he feels the side where you started. Tap the starting point a time or two and say, "I started over here." Drawing while they write often helps.

Recognizing number combinations to ten: Using a 20 x 20 inch square of tagboard, mark it into two-inch squares that progress from one square at the bottom of the first row, to ten squares in the last row. Number the top square in each row. This shows the progression of adding one more.

Then prepare similar strips of squares. Have three or four of the first four strips and duplicates of five through seven. On the side of the strip that is not marked into squares, use a marking pen to write the strip's number. Punch a hole at the top of each strip.

Hang the strip with ten squares on a bulletin board. Hang a shorter strip by it, showing the squares. Have a child decide which second piece should be pinned at the bottom to match the strip with ten squares. When they have practiced counting and matching squares, use the sides that show only the numerals for the more capable students. They may add more than one strip to add to ten. Then see if they can change two of them to one longer strip. If someone added a two to a seven, and then saw he needed one more, he could then be asked how he could change two of them for one longer piece. Have it where children can use it when they choose to do so.

Individualized Written Work

Follow the dots: Make the pictures according to individual abilities. Some would have a need for uncomplicated pictures using less numbered dots to follow, such as a barn with a large door, kite, or a tree in a triangular shape. Others would enjoy the challenge of following dots that require the reading of more numerals in a more complicated picture, such as a house with an extended section, a gabled roof with a chimney, and a door.

Fill in the missing number: According to individual needs and abilities, prepare repeated rows of numbers by omitting different ones in each row. The child is to fill in the numbers that are missing. Some children may be working from one to six, while others can be using double numbers.

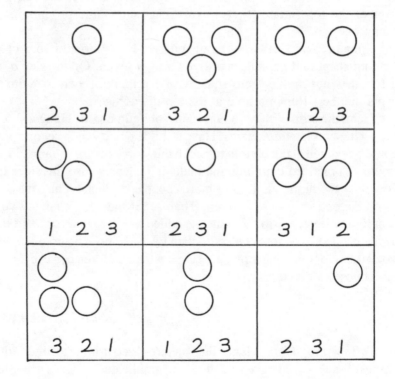

Figure 7-3

Individual matching (Figure 7-3): Be sure the sets are easily identifiable as being separate sets and that the directions for marking the numeral that matches the particular set are understood. The children having problems are often confused as to what they are doing. They have a need for individual guidance.

Figure 7-4 is to mark a set that corresponds with the numeral in that row.

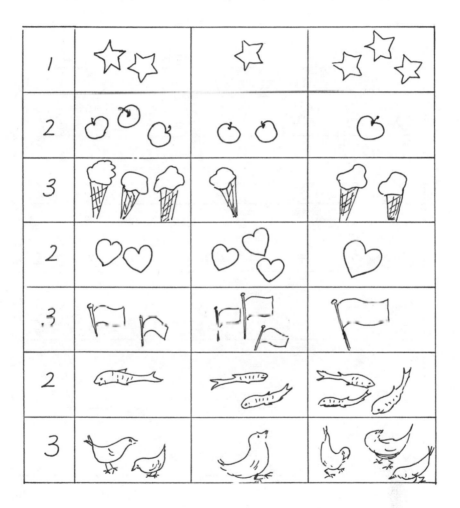

Figure 7-4

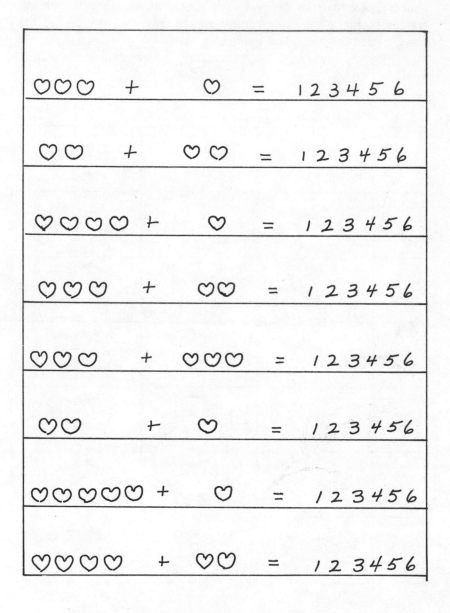

Figure 7-5

2 5 4 3 2 5
   3   1
4 2 5 1 3 4 5
         3   1 5 3
5 2 4 1 5

5

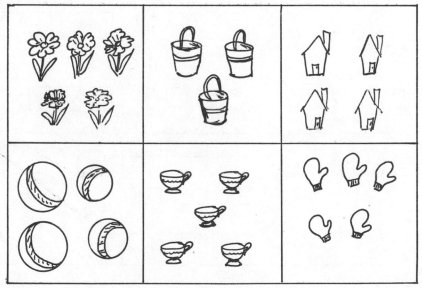

Figure 7-6

99848

8   5   6   3

9   7   8   5   9

6   3   6   9   7

9   4   9   8   4

9

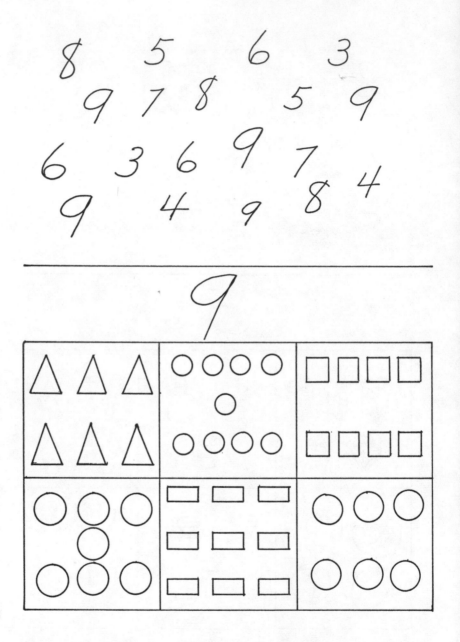

Figure 7-7

Figure 7-5 is for adding sets of objects and marking the numerals.

Figures 7-6 and 7-7 are samples of a way to work with numerals and sets. The indicated numeral is to be marked each time it is found in the group of numerals, practice writing the numeral in the middle space, and mark the sets having that number of objects. This type of work sheet can be made for each numeral.

MAKING THE MATHEMATICS VOCABULARY MEANINGFUL

Many children are unable to solve number problems because they have a poor concept of the words that are used. Directional words, comparative and quantitative terms, and ordinal numbers can cause an inability to perform a certain task when the directions are not understood. It is of paramount importance that all words are understood if proper actions are to result.

Directional Words

Left and right directions should be established early in the year. It is essential to know the directional as well as quantitative words. "Which set has the most?; find the top and the bottom set." "Count the shapes on the upper (lower) part of the paper." "Make the long lines on the sides, and the short lines on the top and bottom." "Put the numbers on the left side, and the shapes on the right side." "Draw a line from the numbers that are above (on the left side of) the line on your paper to the same number that is below (on the right side of) the line on your paper." "Begin writing your numbers at the top, on the left, and write them down (across) the paper," "Make a line above (over), below (under), the set."

Locating places on a paper: Have the children sitting in a group so that their hand responses may be quickly seen. Give each one a piece of paper to place before him. Give directions: "Touch the top of the paper, the bottom, the left side, the right side, the upper left corner, the lower right corner, the center of the paper. Put your finger above the paper, below it, under it, on it, over it. Run your finger across the paper, from left to right, at the top, the middle, the bottom."

Comparative and Quantitative Terms

By using objects, have the children find the largest, the smallest; the tallest (longest), the shortest; the biggest, the littlest; the group with the most, the least; the one that stands highest, the lowest; the big one, the small one; the group that has many, few objects. Use the objects to select not only the superlative amounts, but the majority—most, more; least, less; all, some, few, etc.

This can be used with pictures by having the children draw lines over certain comparative sizes, and circles under their opposites. Be sure the directions are clear and are repeated for each step.

The comparative terms should be a part of the daily vocabulary when talking about seating the tallest or shortest people to see a movie; when using long, longer, or longest blocks for a project; selecting large, small, or smallest pieces of paper for an art project; many, more, or most pieces in a game.

Fractional parts: Children able to understand comparative terms can understand the division of a whole piece into its parts. They learn the term "half" when they see a shape in two equal pieces. They can understand the meaning of one half, and that it is more or less than the whole thing. When they see ½, they learn that an object, or set of objects, is divided into two equal parts.

Show a shape that is cut into two unequal pieces—is one of them one half? Have a set of even-numbered objects. See if they can be divided in half. Try a set with an uneven number of objects. Have children figure how it could be divided in half. What would they do to be sure a stick would be cut in half?

Show the two halves of a shape. Cut each one in half again. Ask the children to tell the number of equal parts there are now. Show the fractional number ¼.

Ordinal Numbers

The ordinal method of counting can be introduced early in the year as a casual method of counting. For the finger game, "Here's a ball," talk about the size of the first, second, and third balls. When the children are getting in a line, or coming for turns, comment about the first one, second one, etc. Any turns or selections afford opportunities to use ordinal counting. The calendar dates are read by ordinal numbers.

To associate the words with the numerals, give numeral cards to a row of children. Ask children to say the names of the children in the row when you say the ordinal number. "What is the name of the third person?" Or give directions to the children holding the cards. "The second and fifth children stoop, the third and fourth ones stretch tall."

A finger game can be used for ordinal counting. Begin the action with the thumb.

> Five little fingers, standing side by side.
> The first one said, "I think that I will hide."
> The second one said, "I think that I should go."
> The third one said, "I hate to break this row."
> The fourth one said, "I can hardly stand."
> The fifth one said, "I'm glad I'm on a hand."
> Closed went the fingers, in a little ball.
> Now they're resting quietly, not a move at all.

CONCLUSION

Children must learn the sequence of counting and the symbols that identify the process. They must acquire the basic concepts of the words that are used. These skills can be advanced during the routine, daily experiences. By using games and planned activities, the mathematical concepts can be applied in meaningful ways to make the use of numbers, their applications, and their computation productive. As small muscle skills develop, children can learn to write their numbers and problems.

All levels of ability must be recognized and served by planning individualized instruction.

Teachers having disadvantaged children will enjoy this book that covers many areas of learning concerning early education, including arithmetic: Bereiter, Carl, and Siegfried Engelmann, *Teaching Disadvantaged Children in the Preschool*, Englewood Cliffs, N.J.: Prentice-Hall, Inc., 1966.

SEEING THE ABCs
THE EASY WAY FOR
EACH INDIVIDUAL

8

Children come to school with varying degrees of enthusiasm for what they will be doing. "Going to school" has been synomynous, for many children, with "learning to read." Eager, more advanced students will be happily anticipating learning experiences when they see the alphabet and words with signs displayed in the room. Others will appear to be unaware of them, depending on their backgrounds.

Children still in the manipulative stage will not show concern for the printed symbols. They should have the opportunity to use kinesthetic letter forms, and have auditory with visual experiences to make the alphabet meaningful.

In this chapter the slower children can have individualized work with "The same or different," "Alphabet song," "Writing the alphabet," "Finding the letters," "Lollipops," "Secret message," "Follow the dots," "Individualized instruction," "Hearing the sounds," "Fill the train," "Charts for sounds," and "Objects."

For more advanced students there are: "Recognizing word forms," "Writing the alphabet," "Lollipops" (also sounds), "Follow the dots" (using all of the alphabet), "Hearing the sounds," "What is it," "Where is the sound," "Combining letter sounds."

ESTABLISHING THE VISUAL CONCEPTS

On the first day, when the group is gathered by you for a short conversation time, identify some of the words that are in the room. Call attention to the calendar or the birthday chart. You may have a traffic sign with the words, STOP—GO, on it. Identify these words as being important to know. Play a brief game by pointing to "Stop" or "Go" to have the children say them when you point to one quickly. Even the less mature children feel pleased about doing this "important reading," as temporary as the learning may be, when you act surprised that they can do this on their first day. When you observe any shy children saying the words, praise them.

After a few group turns for saying the two words, tell them, "Do you know what you have been doing just now? You have been *reading* words! That is what reading is—remembering what these letters say. You surprise me. You are sure this *is* your first day of school?" Then try a few individual turns to say the words. When one of the words has been repeated two or three times, give a shy child a turn, to assure his success. Act pleased and surprised. "With children paying attention and learning, the way you people are doing, I know we are going to have fun this year. You make me so happy to know you." It is an ego building experience, and it helps the children who may have been worrying about what the new situation might bring.

Name cards: Using the name cards, as described in Chapter 4, is a good way to develop an awareness of letter shapes, their grouping, and the need to observe a whole word. Names, such as May and Mary, Tammy and Tommy, must be read carefully. The individual letters become important. Hold the cards one above the other and show the letter differences. Let the children know that they are reading when they are identifying their names.

When the name cards have been generally learned as a group and a child or two may still show difficulty recognizing their names, they should be given two or three minutes to finger trace their cards. This can be done just before the cards are put out to be found, or as a brief individual training during the activity time. Then use three or four names with his card and have him find his own. Praise him for each success.

Writing names: Some children will be ready to write their names when they enter school. Some will have learned only the upper case letters, and will have a need to learn different letter forms. Those who are ready to write their names should have the opportunity to do so. Provide name cards as needed to use as a guide for letter shapes.

For the children having problems, name cards should be made to be felt while finger tracing them. White glue outlines are quickest to make for this tracing. These children should have experiences using wooden letters to make their names. They can also roll ropes of clay to make the letters.

The same or different: Visual concepts of the differences in letter shapes are developed by the use of the activity suggested in Chapter 4—showing groupings of letters to tell whether the two groups are the same or different. Flannel board letters can also be used.

Write different letters on the chalk board, repeating each one several times. Point to one and have others like it found. Use upper case and lower case letters at different times.

Recognizing word forms: Have seasonal pictures on a chart with word labels by them. For Halloween you could have line drawings of a ghost, a cat, a pumpkin, a witch, and the like with the name by each one. Call the labeled pictures to their attention, and have them where they can be observed for two or three days. Have another set of labels. Give turns to try to match the second set with the ones that are on the chart. Children who are ready for more of a challenge can try to match the word with an unlabeled picture.

Have a color chart illustrating each color and its name. Match a duplicate set of color names with the chart. Here, too, the quicker ones will say the color when they see the duplicate cards.

These are just quick, incidental games that are used in the spirit of a game. Praise each successful effort. The set of names could be passed out to give the slower child a few moments to study the card and insure success when his turn comes to match the cards.

Early readers: Just as you do not want to pressure a child with work he cannot do comfortably, you do not want any accelerated child feeling bored. Give accelerated children who show an interest five minutes during an activity time to match and recognize other words. Have many simple pictures with their word names by them and a matching set of names. You could get word ideas from a pre-primer. They may be able to find the words in the book. Keep the time short and lively. Do not have it be a trying task. They may think it is fun for a while and then want to avoid it for a time. This is all right because it is not a scheduled lesson.

Travel game: When the children have practiced matching words that look alike, prepare colored tagboard cards with names of cities or interesting places to visit. Have ten place names, using five colors of tagboard—two different names to one color. The names must be matched from cards of the same color. The ten small cards, using the same names on the same colors, are the tickets.

Show and identify the place names. Arrange them in different places around the room. Ten children draw tickets without being able to see what they get. Give a few moments to study the tickets. When you say "Fly," they are to take off in their airplane for their destination. The colors afford a guide.

This is a popular game, it goes quickly, and is good for a relaxing time.

LEARNING THE LETTER NAMES BY ROTE AND GAMES

All children do not process their information equally well or in the same way. They may have a need for auditory, visual, or tactile experiences. Use various approaches to satisfy individual needs. Here are a few ideas.

Alphabet song: Sing the alphabet song while pointing to the letters. Sing the letters L, M, N, O, P, slowly as this phrase goes so rapidly the letters are not distinct as being letters. At other times have a child point to the letters while the song is sung. For variety, sing the song and stop at any letter. Have a child find the last letter you sang. This requires listening while visually following the letters.

When the song has been used several times, let the children try to catch you in a mistake. Sing rather slowly. Sing the first few letters and then substitute a wrong letter. A child puts up his hand as soon as he hears an error. He must tell the correct letter. Repeat the first letters correctly and make another mistake soon after. They will be paying attention and hearing the sequence of the letters repeatedly. Pretend you are disgusted with yourself. Praise them for being such good listeners. Sing each letter clearly and deliberately.

Writing the alphabet: Begin with the upper case letters. Use one letter at a time to complete some and then to make a row of the letters. The first letter is completed.

Prepare papers with the alphabet letters, omitting a few that are to be filled in. On later papers, omit different letters, increasing the number of omissions each time. Have the complete alphabet at the top of the page for reference to be referred to as it may be needed.

After the upper case letters have been practiced, develop the writing of the lower case letters. Auditory, visual, and tactile experiences will have been continuing at other times so that there will be familiarity with the letter shapes when they are being written.

Arranging the letters: Have the children seated on the floor to have them able to see the wooden letters as facing from left to right. If they are in a circle, some would see the letters in reverse. Have the children take turns putting up one letter at a time in sequential order. Some children may show a need to refer to the alphabet on display. As the letter is placed, the child should say the sentence, "This is ____."

When this skill is developed, have the lower case letters placed to match the upper case letters.

Finding the letters: Write either upper case or lower case letters, making several of each letter. Make them in different sizes. Have turns when you say, "Find me an R." A child finds one and says, "This is an R."

Lollipops to say the alphabet: Using 6-inch paper plates, staple two plates together and then to an ice cream stick or a tongue depressor to look like a large lollipop. With a felt-tip pen, make the upper case letters on one side and the lower case letters on the other. Wrap plastic wrap around the plates and staple it. They are sturdy enough to use for a few years if they are handled properly. Have a bag of candy lollipops as a reward for a child when he can say all of the letter names drawn from the box in random order.

Begin the activity with group participation. It can be used at other times for individual efforts. Have the paper lollipops in a large box. You draw one out at a time, showing the child the upper or lower case letter according to the ones they are learning. Put the letters that are read quickly in one place, and the letters not known, or not sure of, in another. When there are just a few in the "missed" stack, show the child the ones he should work on. The children can get only one reward for saying one side of the lollipops. When he can read all of the upper or lower case letters, he chooses a real lollipop.

Guessing game: Use the kinesthetic letter forms to feel and try to tell the letter by touch. A child, with his eyes covered, or the letter shielded, draws either a card with a letter to trace, or a wooden letter to feel. He tries to identify the letter he has. Some children are aided by feeling the letter while looking at the alphabet.

Secret message: Children having conceptual problems may be aided by trying to get the secret message that is traced on their backs. This is described in Chapter 3. They try to picture the shape you are drawing, and then reproduce it.

Getting turns: At times when you are having children move from where they are, you could tell all the children whose names begin with the letter __ to go. At other times you could say, "The children having the letter __ in their names may go."

Follow the dots: Letters can be used to indicate the sequential order of drawing from dot to dot instead of using numbers. When the alphabet

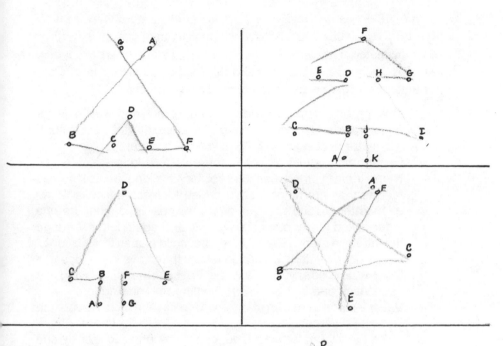

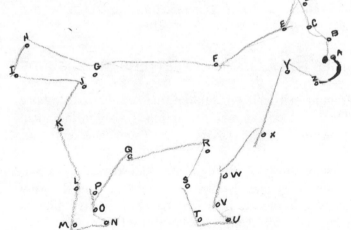

Figure 8-1

is first being practiced, use pictures requiring less letters to know. Gradually add more dots to follow (Figure 8-1).

Individualized instruction: While the children are busy with their activities, five minutes could be used to good advantage on an individual basis if the material is ready. When aides or older students are used, they must know the proper procedures and the results that are desired. They must understand the need for constant encouragement.

1. Making their name: Provide the name outlined with glue for finger tracing. Use arrows to indicate where the lines are to start. It may be necessary to help guide the hand at first.
2. Recognizing letters: Use just three or four letters to identify. Name them in order, then out of order. Use kinesthetic letters to feel as they are named. Give praise for each success. Write each letter several times in different sizes. Find all of the one letter asked for. Another day, review and add a letter. Arrange the letters in order. Place a letter; the child places the next one.
3. Recalling the letters: Using the letters they have learned, say a letter—the child says the next one. Put up the letters leaving one out. Which one is missing? Try writing the missing letter.
4. Use the cards with pairs of letters to identify the pairs that are the same or different.
5. Willie the Worm: When a letter can be recognized quickly and written, the child makes it on a circle to be stapled onto Willie to make him grow. This is described in Chapter 4.

ACTIVITIES FOR ASSOCIATING LETTERS WITH SOUNDS

There must be training in listening if children are to be able to recognize the sounds of letters. Good auditory perception is also an important aspect of speech therapy if a child is to recognize a sound and reproduce it.

Some children have difficulty recognizing letter sounds due to their faulty speech habits. They may use what is commonly called "baby talk." They have not learned to hear the sounds correctly. A child having always said "Tat" for "Cat," or "Wun" for "Run," will have problems and will profit by having a few minutes to practice the sounds. The sound for "s" is one of the last ones children develop. Speech therapists say they are more concerned with this sound after the age of six.

Hearing sounds: When you are teaching a sound, show the letter and tell the sound it makes. Say a few words that have the sound. Use the words that have the sound at the beginning, middle, and the end of the word. Exaggerate your pronunciation to accent the letter and show your mouth and lip action. This is good for individual work.

Make up sentences that emphasize a sound. Have the children say the sentences to note the particular sound, and then to decide which words have it.

C: Carl had a cold and he coughed, c-c-c-c-cough!

G: Get a good gargle. G-g-g-g-gargle.

T: The clock made tiny, ticking sounds, t-t-t-t. (To make the sounds for "t," "d," "n," and "l," the tip of the tongue must go up to the ridge *behind* the teeth. It should not protrude. The lips are spread—not pursed as they would be for "w." Use a mirror to have them see their mouth and tongue action.)

R: Lion really roared. R-r-r-r. (If children substitute "w" for "r," have them smile when they sound the "r." The lips go into the round position for the "w." The mirror will help.)

M: Mary and Mike were eating meat. "M-m-m-m," said Mary. "M-m-m-m," said Mike. "M-m-m-m," they both said. "This is what I like."

H: Henry hauled heavy wood. Then Henry went, "h-h-h-h."

S: Sammy snake was sliding through the grass. He made the sound, sssssssssss.

F: Freddie's frisky cat was feeling cross. He sounded, f-f-f-f-f.

P and B: The sound for "p" is a forcing of the breath from closed lips. The "b" has a vocal sound preceding the opening of the lips. There is not as much force of air as there is for the "p." Have the children start the sound and then open the lips. If the sound is taught as being "buh," it becomes difficult to associate it with any vowel other than "u."

Saying words: When a letter sound is being learned, say a few words that begin with the particular sound as a starter. Then have the children say as many words having the same initial sound as they can. Write the words as they are used. As the skill develops, more words will be said for each sound. Add interest to the challenge by telling them, "You thought of so many words for the letter __, I think you will not get more than __, (a reasonably low number) for this sound today. This letter sound is not as easy for you. I just don't think you can beat me today.'' They rise to the challenge and become surprisingly able to think of unusual words.

Then have them make the letter (or give papers with the letter made) and draw a picture of one of the words that begins with the letter. With the joy of having bettered your challenges, even the slower children are apt to continue to think of more words. As long as you maintain control while giving the children the feeling that they are doing more than was expected of them, they will happily keep trying.

What is it?: Play a guessing game using beginning sounds. Identify a sound and give clues that will lead to the answer for the question, "What is it?" Some suggestions follow.

S: 1. It is something you wear on your feet. (socks)
   2. It is something that makes your face look happy. (smile)
   3. Everyone has it. It covers all of you. (skin)
   4. It is warm and bright. (sun)
T: 1. You use it when you talk. (tongue)
   2. You use them when you eat. (teeth)
   3. They are on your feet. (toes)
   4. You do your work on one. (table)

Where is it?: The same idea for "What is it" can be used to associate initial sounds with articles in the room. Show a letter and have the sound identified. Give clues that relate to the objects that are to be found, or ask for anything in the room that begins with a particular sound.

D: 1. Girls wear them. (dresses)
   2. We open it at times. (door) (drawer)
   3. They are in the playhouse. (dolls) (dishes)

It is sound perception that is being developed, not spelling. A child may say ceiling for the sound of s, or phonograph for the "f." They should not be confused by telling them that other letter combinations are used.

Where is the sound?: Use pictures that have the desired sound at the beginning, middle, or at the end of the word. Have a child say one of the words, and then decide where the sound came in the word. For the sound of B, you could have such pictures as: bat, ball, book, tub, crab, web, rubbers, cabbage, marbles. For S: sandwich, soap, bus, grass, whistle, basket.

Treasure hunt: After some of the sounds have been practiced and some skill is developed, have a treasure hunt involving two or three of the sounds. Use pictures from the sets used previously and spread them around in the circle. Two or three children, according to the number of sounds being sought, try to collect pictures that have their sound some place in the word. The game is to see which one collects the most treasure. Some pictures may include more than one of the sounds.

Fill the train: A train can be made by using boxes with wooden spools for wheels, to be fastened together with long paper fasteners. Each boxcar would have a letter on its side and be added, one at a time, as the letter sound was being developed.

The train could also be made by mounting a picture of an engine. The boxcars can be made by gluing on pieces of paper or envelopes so that each car, labeled with a letter, can be a pocket to hold pictures.

While one sound is being learned, the children are asked to find magazine pictures that begin with the sound. The pictures are shown to the group and the words repeated before they go into their proper car. They should be used for an occasional review of the sounds.

Charts for sounds: Label a chart with a letter. Children find pictures beginning with the sound to have it pasted on the chart. The charts can be used for a quick review of sounds.

Which letter is it?: Instead of saying a letter name and having it found by a child, say the letter sound to have the letter selected. The child holding the letter says the sound when he says, "This is __."

Using objects: Put out several objects or pictures that have different beginning letter sounds. You may have such things as: ball, book, box, button, basket; the number 2, truck, tree, train; soap, scissors, stapler, star, sponge, etc. Having turns, ask a child to find the object that begins with a certain sound. The child less sure may select an object already named. If the sound is correct, he should be praised for the selection. Or, have a child select an object, say its name, and then say the beginning sound. This is also mentioned for auditory discrimination.

Lollipops for sounds: Using the same lollipop forms for letter recognition, hold them one at a time, to have the letter sounds said. The vowel sounds are correct if the long sound can be said. Some children will be able to say all or most of the sounds. Some will be able to say only a few. For these children, show them the lollipops they could say, and praise them for knowing them.

WAYS TO HELP ADVANCED STUDENTS COMBINE LETTER SOUNDS

When the sounds of the letters are being learned, mount just the vowels, using lower case letters. Have the letters said and tell the children these letters are called vowels and that they can say their own names and they may also say other sounds. Have the symbols for the short sound above each vowel. Explain that the mark means the letter is making a different sound. Even though they are on display and are explained to the group, only the children who are ready for this step will absorb their differences. The others will benefit from them according to the degree that they are ready. They may learn that these letters are vowels, but they may not be ready to differentiate the differences between the long and short sounds.

You can make story ideas to associate visual, oral, and auditory perceptions. According to your own situation, these stories for the short sounds can be presented to the group for a first general introduction, and then used later during a five or ten minute period for more instruction with the children who can handle it.

Story ideas: Make a set of individual vowels with the diacritic symbols. Use one vowel for a session with a small group.

   a: A boy saw something that looked as though it would be good to eat. He did not know what it was, but he put it in his mouth anyway. It was not good. It was very bitter. He opened his mouth and said ă-ă-ă.
   e: A little old man could not hear very well. He was getting rather deaf. When someone talked to him, and he could not hear what was said, he put a hand by his ear, and said, "ĕ"?
   i: Baby could not talk. When he saw something that he wanted, he put out his hands and said, ĭ-ĭ-ĭ.
   o: The children had been hiking. They had walked for a

long time. When they got home they each found a comfortable place to rest, and said, ŏ-ŏ-ŏ.

   u: Randy and Ronny were playing with a big heavy ball. They were trying to toss it to each other to catch it. Randy forgot to toss it one time and threw it too hard. Ronny could not catch the ball. Instead, it landed against his stomach, and he said, "ŭ."

After each vowel presentation, write the vowel several times in different sizes. Have the children make the vowel sound as you point to the letters.

Have several pictures of objects that require the use of the vowel sound. The children say the words and try to hear the vowel sound. Put up some pictures including a few that do not have the one sound being studied. The children try to find the ones with the particular sound.

Combining sounds: When a vowel sound is learned, write it and also a consonant. Using "a" and "t," have each sound identified. Then tell them you are going to slide your finger from one letter to the other. They are to continue the first sound until you get to the "t," when they will make that sound. Go slowly a few times. Then tell them you will be going faster and faster, and they are to make the sounds following your finger. When it is repeated rapidly without a pause, they get the sounds blending without accenting the final consonant. Use other consonants.

Initial consonants: Write one of the letter combinations that has been practiced. Tell them you are now going to put a letter that is to be sounded before they say the little word. You will slide your finger from the first sound to the word they know to see what new word it will make. Identify each sound before it is added. With the word "at," begin with the sounds that can be held, such as m, s, f, or r. They will be better able to combine them to become words. The explosive sounds (p, b, c, etc.), will be easier to combine when you move your finger rapidly, when they realize what they are doing. Quickly go over the new words they have made.

At another session, use a different ending combination: an, ad, etc.

When they are enjoying making words, add a bit of fun by telling them you will write a sentence they can read. Choose some of the words from the list you have written. It might be pat fat cat. Or, fat cat ran; fat cat had sad dad mad.

The children who are early readers will be glad to share some time

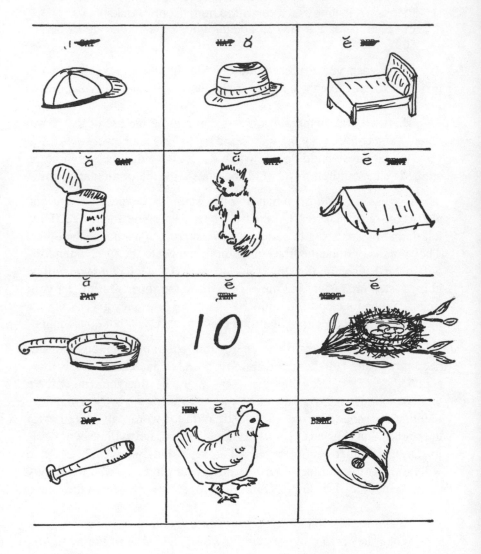

Figure 8-2

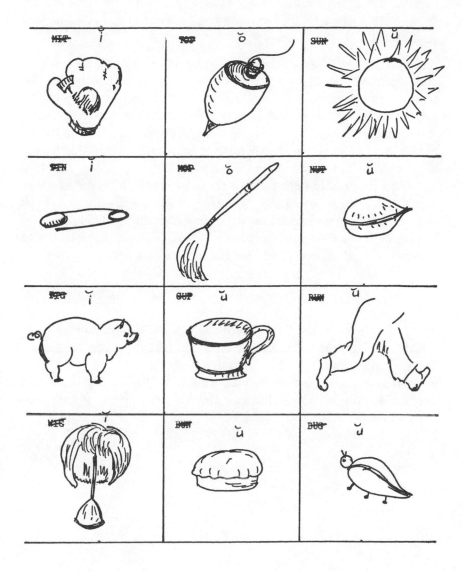

Figure 8-3

from an activity period to work on word sounds. A few others often ask to join the group part of the time. They get what they can and show when they have reached their limit. Occasionally a child surprises you by being quite adept with the sounds when he had not indicated he was ready for it.

Spelling words: Once they have learned to sound and read words, children enjoy making lists of words to keep. Ditto the consonants and vowels. Have them in individual envelopes or bowls where they can be located easily by the working group. Ditto easily recognized pictures that are to be selected by individual choice. The picture is to be pasted onto a large piece of paper. Then the proper letters are pasted by the picture to spell the word (Figures 8-2 and 8-3).

This is ready to be used as a chosen activity, to make as many words as they care to try. The very capable children will want to do most of them. It becomes a concentrated working situation where children are helping each other sounding words and letters. The spelling may not be accurate—''bel'' is acceptable for the picture of a bell.

SUMMARY

There must be opportunities to see the letters and their combined uses. Children should learn the letter names and that there are sounds associated with them, according to individual abilities.

Daily procedures must be planned that will allow for individual needs and skills in order to have all children progressing at their own rates and abilities.

DEVELOPING
THE VOCABULARY

9

To assure optimal learning opportunities, not only must there be a learning atmosphere, a program that is planned to recognize individual sensory input needs, and many individualized activities to accommodate these various needs, but you must be certain that the words used are understood in context. Individual past experiences affect the vocabulary each child has when he comes to school.

Children with limited backgrounds have a need for enrichment through vicarious experiences. These must be provided through stories, poems, pictures, activities, and conversations. Class-related experiences are valuable for them. Sharing and observing pets, observing nature around the school, going for walks or special visits, and seeing subject-oriented movies can enrich their backgrounds for expression and understanding.

Before you can individualize instruction, you must know the children's needs. Two tests for word concepts have been suggested in Chapter 2. When you are aware of individual needs, you can teach *to* them.

Activities in this chapter can be used in a group situation while directing questions according to ability. The suggestions that are helpful for slower children are: "Parents' help," "Creating stories from drawings," "Class stories," "Using a puppet," "Finger games," and "Tactile experiences." For more advanced students: "Creating original stories," "Using a puppet," "Finish the story," "Substituting words," and "Using words with opposite meanings."

SUGGESTIONS FOR WAYS TO EXTEND THE VOCABULARY

Hearing and Creating Stories

Parents' help: The use and concept of words can be greatly extended by the regular hearing of stories and poems. When parents ask, as they so often do, how they can help at home, ask them to read to their children daily. Encourage them to go to the public library where they can be helped with their selections. The parents of the children showing the greatest needs may not use stories that are suitable, or at the proper level. They may not realize that the librarians will help them with their selections. Parents should provide books for the children to handle and generally enjoy.

Stories: Some stories can be told without the use of a book. Other stories have been written so well that they should be read in order to get every word the author has expressed so graphically. Some authors paint pictures with their words. Good pictures, accompanying a story, do much to create mental images and aid the understanding of the words. A few illustrated books that should be read rather than told include:

Make Way for Ducklings, Robert McCloskey. The Viking Press, N.Y., 1961.

One Morning in Maine, Robert McCloskey. The Viking Press, N.Y., 1961.

Blueberries for Sal, Robert McCloskey. The Viking Press, N.Y., 1952.

The Little House, Virginia Lee Burton. Houghton Mifflin Co., 1942.

The Story About Ping, Marjorie Flack and Kurt Wiese. The Viking Press, N.Y., 1933.

Little Lamb's Curls, Polly Miller Mc Millan. Lothrop Publishing Co., 1962.

These are a few of the many books that seem to be becoming classics in children's literature. Any librarian can suggest more.

A book that is intended for very young children, or for children who have a need to develop good auditory perception and retention habits, is *The Headstart Book of Looking and Listening*, Shari Lewis, Jacquelyn Reinach. McGraw-Hill Book Company, 1966.

If you feel a need for a very quiet, relaxing period, a book that is excellent and should be read rather slowly with a quiet voice is: *Sleepy Forest*, Naoma Zimmerman. Children's Press, Chicago, 1955.

There should be a regularly scheduled story time in the school day. It is one period that should have its time each day if it is possible. The stories can be planned to relate to seasonal interests, room activities, or selected just for their literary value and the pleasure they afford. Have a library corner where the children can have time to enjoy the books on their own. Afford opportunities for them to select favorite books to read to the class.

Creating original stories from pictures: Some pictures invite creative imagination by what they portray. It may be the facial expressions, or the actions and objects that are pictured. Pictures can be found in magazines or discarded books.

Show a picture and have the children study it. Ask them to think about what might have happened to cause the person or animal to appear as he does and what might have happened first to have the things pictured the way they are. Then think about what might be being said, or thought about, according to the picture. What do they think could be going to happen next. Encourage different opinions to have the interpretations individually creative. Ask them to pretend to be what is being portrayed, and to express the thoughts or words that could have happened. They become more expressive when not talking in the third person.

Some children seem to have no difficulty when creating stories. Others, having had little experience with imaginative activities, have a need for guiding assistance. Rather than having them plan an entire story, give one thought at a time for a response. "What do you think might have happened to have —— look this way?" "What do you think —— might be thinking (saying) now?" "What will be said (happen) next?'' The suggestions can be quickly jotted down, or a tape can be run as children respond.

When the story has been completed, play or read it back. They might decide to make changes. Have the children listen for and identify words or expressions that helped to make the story more enjoyable.

Creating stories from drawings: Furnish drawing paper that has a line drawn, leaving space at the bottom of the page for a story. Children draw their pictures and then dictate the story that is to be written in the space that is provided. Some of the stories will be only one or two sentences; others will be much longer, according to individual abilities. This is a good way to encourage the children who are less inclined to compose stories. They are more apt to tell about their own creations than they are to try to imagine a story about another person's picture. Their story sentences may be more enumerative: ''This is a house,'' ''There is a boy,'' etc. Encourage them to tell what might be going to happen that you cannot see.

Class stories: You may want to use a form of a newsletter to send home as a report of the work being done. The group decides on the interesting things that they have been doing to tell about in the letter. If there is more than one activity—art, building, a trip, etc.—explain that they will discuss one thing at a time to keep it interesting. Write their ideas. Read them back for corrections or additions. When the children have approved their reports, have the stories dittoed to have each child take one home.

This can be a good end-of-the-year project in story composition. The children can tell about their favorite activities in kindergarten, the events they remember best or enjoyed the most. There could be a report on ''Our Favorite Stories,'' or ''Songs We Enjoyed.'' A previous class story, or individual original poems or short stories can be included. If space is provided when the sheets are dittoed, each child can illustrate some of the sections before taking it home.

Using a puppet: If you use a puppet for dramatic actions, it can draw out many shy children to talk. The shy children may have a need for the puppet to ask a question and then to have them respond. The more they can identify the puppet with its personification of being a friend, the easier it is for them to respond.

The puppet can be used when special words are being learned. He might say, "There is a big word that I like. I like the way it sounds and I like what it means. The word is 'patient.' I see children being patient when waiting for a turn. I must be patient while I wait to visit with you. Can someone tell me what it means to be patient?" Usually some children will try to give their idea of the word. If they have difficulties have the puppet help them.

"I will use the word in a sentence, then I will ask someone else to make a sentence with the word 'patient.' "

"I must be patient when I am waiting for a turn to talk."

When the responses get started, the ideas extend to "waiting for Christmas," "waiting for my birthday," "waiting for summer to come," and the like.

The same idea can be used at other times with other words that will become a part of (at least some) vocabularies—enormous, unusual, huge, pleasant, curious, etc. Learning the words can be fun when it is done as a game with a friend. At times have the puppet suddenly ask about a word that had been used previously, as a surprise question. It maintains the spirit of fun if the puppet is made to play his part well, acting surprised and happy when a word meaning is recalled.

Retelling stories: Provide opportunities for children to tell a favorite story to the class. The story may be one that has been read to the group, or a story the child knows. Children less able to express themselves may tell nursery rhymes or short versions of a story.

Finish the story: You can begin a story by introducing a situation and having the children furnish their ideas to continue the story.

"Mother dog told her two puppies to stay in the yard to play. She showed her puppies the fence, and told them it was there to keep them from danger. (Ask what 'danger' means. Direct your questions to avoid getting all the responses from the more articulate children.) One puppy was named Frisky, because he was so lively. ('How do you think he acted if he was lively?') The other puppy was named Floppy, because his long ears flopped down.

"Mother dog called her puppies to come for their afternoon nap. Mother dog was tired—she had been busy—and she curled up to rest. Floppy was tired, and he flopped by mother dog. Frisky wiggled around to lie down, but he did not feel like napping. Soon Mother dog and

Floppy were asleep, but Frisky was still wiggling. Frisky listened to the quiet breathing of Mother dog and Floppy. The more he tried to lie quietly, the more he wiggled. Then he thought, 'I'll get up and take a short walk.'

"Frisky walked around the yard. He walked by the fence. What did he do?"

Have children finish the story according to their own ideas.

"The class was making gifts for their mothers. They could choose what they wanted to make. Marni liked to use ceramic clay and put a shiny glaze on it. She wanted to make something that would look pretty and feel pleasant to hold. ('How would it feel to be pleasant?')

"Milly liked to paint. She wanted to make something bright that her mother would enjoy.

"When their gifts were finished, and carefully wrapped, they brought them home. Marni's mother talked about the way her gift felt to her hands, and how she would use it. Milly's mother talked about the colors of her gift, and where she would put it.

"Tell what each mother said so we can guess what each gift might have been, and how it might have looked."

Using Poems

Poetry is often neglected. It should be introduced at an early age and used regularly to be appreciated. Poems have an appeal because of their rhythm, their rhyme, and for the descriptive words they may use. When children hear poetry often, many are able to create their own poems. Nursery rhymes are commonly used and enjoyed. Other poems can be enjoyed when the children have opportunities to hear them.

It is an advantage to have a collection of poems readily available. Favorite ones can be mounted on cards. A suitable picture will help to identify the poem. Children can have turns to select and identify one of the cards to be "The Poem for the Day." The card and the child's name are put in the special place for when it is to be read. An excellent collection of poems is *Poems and Rhymes*, Childcraft—The How and Why Library Volume 1. Field Enterprise Educational Corporation, Chicago. It contains more than 275 traditional and modern poems.

Finger games: Easy to learn rhyming verses are used with finger activities, or they can be used with flannelboard objects. Being related to activities of immediate interest and dramatized, the rhymes are rather readily learned. The actions help to make the words meaningful, providing the possibility for new words, or different uses of words to be incorporated into the vocabulary. Children too shy to talk alone before the group feel more relaxed and secure when they participate in group speaking.

Rhymes for Fingers and Flannelboards, Louise Binder Scott and J. J. Thompson, McGraw Hill, Inc., 1966, has rhymes that are suitable for the many activities that are of interest to the young children. Finger actions are described and suggestions for the use of the flannelboard are offered.

Two other excellent books are: *Listen! And Help Tell the Story*, Bernice Wells Carlson, Abingdon Press, New York, and *Let's Do Fingerplays*, Marion Grayson, Robert B. Luce, Inc., Washington.

Finger games can be created for brief relaxation.

My fingers wiggle all around. (Both hands opened wide, and fingers wiggling.)
Then I give a clap. (Give a clap.)
Now my hands shake loosely, and I put them on my lap.
(Arms forward, hands dangle to shake.)

A longer relaxing poem is:

Time for work, and time for play,
    This has been a busy day.
Now I know that I should rest,
    To help my body feel its best.
I will be a soft rag doll,
    And not a bone I'll have, at all.
My head drops down, my arms hang loose,
    My back feels like some runny juice.
My legs won't hold me straight and tall,
    They're letting me slide into a ball.
Here I am all in a heap,
    I'll just pretend I'm fast asleep.
It feels so good to just let go,
    From the top of my head to the tip of my toe.
I'll count slowly, one—two—three,
    I pop up rested. Quiet me.

Say the rhyme while the children go through the actions. As it is learned by different repetitions, children can help with the rhyme.

A finger game that includes less commonly used words: snuggled, startled, creeping, silently, stole, is enjoyed for its ending. Explain that one hand closed into a fist with the thumb under the fingers is a mouse hole with the mouse inside. The other hand is to be the cats.

Holding one hand to one side to be the mouse in its hole, begin the rhyme.

Here is Mrs. Tabby Cat, *(hold up the other thumb)*
And her little kittens *(hold up four fingers)*
Curled up on their little bed *(fold fingers and thumb together)*
Snuggled with some mittens.
They were startled by a squeak, *(Mouse pops out of his hole and wiggles)*
Their heads popped up to see. *(hand being cats pops partly open)*
Kittens, I think that's a mouse. Now just follow me. *(hushed voice)*
Creeping, creeping, creeping on, silently they stole. *(fingers undulating as crawling toward the mouse)*
Just before the cats got there, the mouse popped in his hole. *(Mouse-thumb pops back into hole just before the cats arrive)*

Say the rhyme first. Ask questions to guide the children's thinking about the meaning of the words they may not understand. When the meanings of the words are understood, their repetitions will help to incorporate them into the children's vocabularies.

Whether it is a story, poem, or song, be certain the meanings of words are clear. I recall enjoying the old song, "Flow Gently Sweet Afton," but being very puzzled by the phrases, "Thou wild-winging blackbirds, Thy screaming forbear." It did not make sense that a bird should be screaming for a bear. The day the word "forbear" was learned, the phrase had a new meaning, and the song made sense. A child may be able to use a word correctly in a previously used context. This could be recall rather than an understanding of the word's meaning. There are words that sound alike, but have different meanings. They can confuse the children with limited vocabularies. ("The man went to *sea*," "That was a *hoarse* sound," "There is a *pair* of *pears* on the table," "The shoes are in *pairs*.")

Any material presented to the children should be critically pre-read to catch words that could possibly have different meanings for the children. The level and ability of each group will determine the material used.

At times, ask the children to close their eyes to "see" what the words tell them because, "Sometimes we can see more with our eyes closed and we are imagining the picture." Have them describe the picture they imagined. Many poems and songs are more appreciated when they create mental images. The words become more meaningful, and some of their descriptions become quite fanciful.

Substituting words: Words are being substituted when stories are dramatized and words for the parts are not learned. If a story has been presented in an interpretive way, it will be easier for the children to become the characters and then to use their own words. Children with limited vocabularies should be encouraged and praised for all their efforts. There may be a need to explain some situations or expressions in the story to make certain the children have the right concept of what they are to be doing.

Using different words that express the same meaning helps to enlarge and strengthen the vocabulary they already have. Create a short story or some sentences using words that will be replaced by substitute words. For example (the italicized words are to be substituted):

Suzy was a *cheerful* girl.
It was getting late and I felt *drowsy*.
The plants in my garden grew *rapidly*.
The birds flew *above* the trees.
Mother cat did not want anyone to *annoy* her babies.

The italicized words are to be rephrased. Let the children know that you will stop to have them use other words for one of the words you will use, and that you will let them know which word you want to have changed and still mean the same thing. Accent the word to be substituted, or use a gesture.

We went for a ride in the country. Some cars on the road were going *fast*. They were _____. (Give several opportunities to offer words or phrases.) We saw a mountain that had very *big* rocks. The rocks were _____. There was a field of *pretty* flowers. They looked _____. We stopped to take a walk. There were *small* flowers growing close to the ground. They were quite ____. We walked to some trees and saw a chipmunk with his cheeks *stuffed* with nuts. His cheeks were ____. He chattered at us and it seemed to us he was saying, *"Halt."* He wanted us to ____. We watched him a little while and then we *continued* our walk. We wanted to ____. Under the trees we began to feel *cold*. We were ____. It was time to *stop* our walk. It was time for it to ____. We *liked* the things we saw. We ____ them. Our walk was so long that our feet began to *ache*. They felt ____. It made us feel *glad* to get back into the car. On the way home we did not have to *pause* at all. It was a *good* day.

Jot down the suggestions and reread the story that includes the synonymous phrases.

Saying the same thing in a different way: Explain to the children that you will make up some make-believe happenings and will say what a person might have said. You will want the children to try to "see" in their minds what was described. Repeat the quotation and ask for ways it could be said differently using other words and still mean the same thing. Just as children having problems need individual help, more gifted children may need their own time if the rate of the class is well below theirs. These sentences may be more suitable for them.

1. We saw a grove of trees. All of the trees, except one, were about the same size. John said, "One tree is taller than the others."
2. Mary and Bob were taking a walk near some hills. Mary said, "See that very big boulder." (Determine their understanding of "boulder.")
3. The family had worked hard making a flower garden. When it was blooming, Mother said, "The flower garden looks pretty."
4. It was a warm day, hundreds of bugs had just hatched and came flying out from their nest through a hole in the ground. Joe called to his friend, "Look at all the very, very small bugs in the air."
5. You could see the trees bending and swaying. The noise the wind was making was very loud. Betty said, "The wind is blowing very hard."
6. Jim was going to the doctor's office to have a shot. Jim knew that if he sat quietly while he had his shot it would help the doctor and the shot would not hurt too much. He said, "I know what it is, and I'm not scared."
7. An old house had some work done on it, and then it was painted. When Billy went by it he said, "That house does not look the same."

Using a suitable word: Tell the children that you will say a sentence that tells them something. Then you will say a part of another sentence and they will think of a word that tells what the first sentence meant.

1. The hole went far down. It was ____.
2. Mary always said "please" when she wanted something. She was ____.
3. The ground was a little wet. When we sat down it felt ____.
4. The man could not hear. He was ____.
5. That box does not look the same as it was. It looks ____.
6. John was not afraid. He was ____.
7. The children wondered about what was in the package. They were ____.
8. When they saw the parts of the toy that had to be put together, they still did not know what it was. They were ____.
9. She waited quietly for her turns without fussing. She was ____.
10. I think you are right. I ____ with you.
11. The children were having great fun at the party. They felt ____.

Tactile experiences to suggest words: Have an assortment of objects that have different textures and degrees of hardness. A child selects one and says a word that can help to describe the way it feels. It is passed to another child who may add a different word. When no more words can be thought of for that object, have someone select another. Ask the group if they agree with the suggested descriptive words.

Visual experiences to create words: Show pictures—one at a time—that have some dramatic or emotional impact. Ask the children to pretend that the picture is real, and that they are in it. Have them think of a word that would tell how they would feel. Offer turns to the less aggressive children first. The more often they can contribute words, even very ordinary ones, the more confidence they have, making it more possible for them to absorb words that are new to them. When it seems that all the words that are possible for the group to offer have been given, show a different picture that expresses another mood.

Auditory experiences: Unexpected or routine sounds can offer an opportunity to use descriptive words. Rain on the windows may bring out words such as pattering, tapping, dripping, and splashing. Thunder often frightens children. If they listen for it and try to think of words to describe it, the distracting activity can take away some of their tension.

They can learn that thunder is just noise, and that they should not be afraid of noises. When children have some understanding of an electric storm, and that the noise is caused by the sudden expansion of the air when the hot lightning has passed through it, they have less fear of the noise. They can hear the noise a balloon or a bag makes when the air rushes out.

When playing records just for listening or that the children might interpret with movements, ask them to tell what the music causes them to feel. Have them try to describe it in one word if they can.

Say some words and ask whether they make them think of loud or soft things, heavy or light things: crash, roar, tinkle, ring, thud, boom, puff, whisper, bang, plop, pop, buzz, jingle, grind, patter, drip, and so on. The ideas suggested may vary according to experiences.

USING WORDS WITH OPPOSITE MEANINGS

As children develop their vocabularies, they can understand the meaning of "opposite" when examples are given. Games using opposite words are more fun when they are used later in the year after there has been more vocabulary development.

Toss them out: Having the group in a circle, "toss" a word to each one in turn. He is to "toss" back its opposite word. Knowing your group's individual abilities, say easier words for the children who need them, and more difficult ones for the more advanced children. Maintain the attitude of a game with happy anticipation and a smile or a praise for each correct response. Have a list of words prepared with different degrees of difficulty. Here are some suggested words, using either one of a pair:

in - out	big - little	out - in
up - down	wet - dry	laugh - cry
yes - no	fast - slow	hard - soft
high - low	happy - sad	tall - short
hot - cold	fat - thin	big - little
last - first	over - under	stop - go
open - close	light - dark	heavy - light
white - black	sharp - dull	more - less
long - short	shiny - dull	smooth - rough
many - few	same - different	noisy - quiet
good - bad	near - far	laughing - crying

Use one word one time, and the opposite word for other turns. The more frequently the words are used, the more they are apt to be usable. When a child can say the opposite of a word, it indicates that he understands the meaning of both.

CONCLUSION

The vocabulary is being developed in every activity of the day. It is essential for the teacher to be constantly aware of any words that might confuse some children. The words may occur in a story, a song, or a discussion of the work that has been done. It is necessary to provide vicarious experience to assure a background for the desired vocabularies. It is also necessary to try to incorporate new words with their meanings in the conversation when the occasion presents itself.

The use of words in a rote form of recall does not mean that the words' meaning is understood. There must be different ways for the words to be used to indicate an understanding of their meanings in context.

The children should have mental and sensory experiences to develop the meanings of words and have them become useful. When the spirit of a game or pleasure is added, learning is easier. Individual abilities and needs must be considered in each assigned request to instill confidence and a willingness to try in each child. It is essential to show appreciation for all efforts, and a faith in the children's ability to produce.

CREATING
IN ART

10

Art appreciation should be a continuing process. This could be accomplished by room displays and arrangements, and comments about color, shape or form concerning children's work. Observe nature with its shapes and colors. Stimulate observations and free discussions when viewing pictures or any creative work. Encourage creativity and originality in all of the art forms.

A teacher needs many ideas to develop the skills necessary for using the various media. Individual expression is encouraged by learning different ways to use the materials and then to apply that skill to individual creations. Creative art is individual. Therefore, beyond the instruction in the handling of materials, all the suggestions are for individual creations, regardless of the number working in one area.

Children enjoy making special seasonal projects. Some of these are more directed than being creative art. Following directions is a part of learning. As long as this type of lesson is not considered to be developing creative art, and is only a small supplement for the use of art materials, it is legitimate. The skills learned can be applied later to individual creations.

Observing pictures: Learning the way people express themselves through art is aided by the use of good pictures. Have a collection of pictures that includes a variety of subject matter and moods. Showing the way lines and the use of colors can express feelings helps the children project their feelings when they make a picture. A flat or rolling line indicates quietness; a line dashing upward is dynamic. You can demonstrate this by telling the group, "I am thinking of two different things. One is about a quiet time in the evening. Working time is over. The birds have gone to sleep. Soon, people will be going to bed. The other thing I am thinking about is a storm. Trees are bending! Waves are splashing! Things are blowing all around! Now which of these line pictures shows the quiet picture and which one shows the storm?" Make straight and wavy lines on one page. On the other draw quick, stabbing lines that dash up at angles. Children understand the moods of the lines when they can relate to them in some way. The same idea can be used to show subdued colors and brilliant ones.

When you show a picture to the group, do not indicate an opinion of your own. This is to avoid getting responses that merely agree. Ask how the picture makes them feel; does it seem to be a happy or a sad picture, an exciting or a quiet one. When their opinions are accepted as being valid, the children are more apt to try to interpret the picture. Ask what there is about the picture that gives this feeling. Would they like to see something changed in the picture? What colors would they use if they wanted to make a similar picture?

Getting into the spirit of the work: To be able to communicate through art, there must be an understanding and feeling for the project. If there is to be a circus mural with clowns, by merely supplying materials and asking for a picture of a clown, you may get some that resemble clowns. Most of the drawings will be routine drawings of people. Instead, have the children talk about clowns, tell about the ones they have seen, and share laughter about the clowns' funny actions and clothes. Show pictures of clowns, as some may not have seen them. Then have children take turns being clowns. They first describe the way they feel they are painted and dressed, and then go through some clown antics. Immediately after this, have the pictures made while they are still enjoying the mood. There will be delightful clown pictures, full of action and color. While the pictures are being drawn, walk around, and briefly hold up a picture to show funny expressions or vivid colors. This is a good boost for a child who might be expressing himself freely for the first time.

On a day when you can be out of doors for drawing, have the children bring their crayons, a paper, and a piece of cardboard for support. Select a suitable place for them to sit. Then have them close their eyes and tell them to pretend that they have not been able to see for a long time. They do not know what is around them. It is like being blind. When they open their eyes they are to draw the first thing that makes them glad that they can see. It may be something very small, close by, or any first thing they are glad to be able to see.

IDEAS FOR USING PAPER, SCISSORS, PASTE, CRAYONS, AND CHALK

Paper and Scissors

In a situation where many children are moving about while scissors are being used, it is necessary to establish protective rules. Whether the scissors have rounded ends or pointed ones, injuries could result if a child moves around the room carrying the scissors with its blades open, or the ends pointing up. A child can move about in safety while carrying scissors if he holds them in a closed fist, with the blades pointing to the floor. Some children may have a need to be taught the way to hold the scissors for cutting.

Cutting circles: Cutting circles for traffic signals affords a means to introduce the techniques for using scissors. Have squares of paper in the necessary colors. When you are ready to demonstrate the way it is to be done, tell the children the paper is to be a piece of cheese, and the scissors are to be a mouse. These scissor mice are funny because they eat only corners. They do not like long pieces. The mice are hungry, so the first corners they eat are big ones. As a corner is cut, add interest with some appropriate comments, such as, "Um-m-m, that was good. There is another fat corner." When all four corners have been cut, the mouse is not as hungry, but he just cannot leave a corner. The paper is turned as the eight little corners are "eaten." By snipping off the tiny corners, the paper becomes quite round.

Using this method avoids the cutting of spirals that is done so frequently. The same method is used when any round or oval shapes are needed. The children should have a sufficient supply of square or rectangular pieces to allow for the many mistakes that happen while learning.

Scissors that have their blades reversed for left-handed children are available. Many left-handed children have known nothing but frustration when trying to do cutting because they were using scissors made for right-handed people.

When children have the use of scissors, they should have access to paper in a variety of sizes, including a box of colored scraps. Gift wrapping, colored pages from magazines, textured paper, or any similar pieces that might inspire creativity should be included.

Paste

Some teachers use small jars for paste. The lids must be securely in place when the paste is not in use. A satisfactory and paste-saving method is to have a box of butcher paper squares. A small amount of paste, enough for one or two children, can be dipped from a gallon jar. The unused paste is scraped back into the jar.

The first few times paste is used, directions must be repeated and demonstrated to emphasize using one finger tip for pasting. A small amount of paste is spread smoothly along the edge of the paper, leaving no lumps of paste. Show the way to press or rub the pasted pieces to have them adhere. Provide each child with a piece of paper towel or toilet paper to wipe the paste from his fingers.

Torn paper: Tearing paper to create forms offers opportunities for free expression. The children should experiment with paper tearing by making small tears while turning the paper. They may get very small pieces or large pieces. Then, by trying to put the pieces together in different ways, they may decide on some interesting composition to paste onto a large paper. If you demonstrate the activity, you could try to pin the pieces to a flannelboard, adjusting and changing them to show the group how to plan their arrangements. Trees, landscapes, free-form compositions, designs, or many other original ideas will be the result. A teacher's picture should not be left on display because it will cause copying.

Colored strips: Different widths of colored strips of paper may inspire ideas for bending, looping, overlapping, or twisting and pasting them in many ways. The strips may also be used as outlines for pictured objects. When showing the strips to the children, take a minute or two to demonstrate some ways they can be bent, looped, or folded as a starter.

Geometric shapes: Using geometric shapes that have been pre-cut from colored papers affords a means for individual creations. There should be a large supply of each shape cut into different sizes in a variety of colors. Each set of shapes should be in designated boxes to keep the geometric figures separate. Black construction paper as a background affords good contrast for bright colors. Take a few minutes to demonstrate possible ways to create a composition. While arranging your pieces, call attention to colors that show good contrast. Show how shapes in very similar hues are difficult to recognize when they are together. Explain the need for applying the paste around the edges of the pieces instead of putting it in the center. The demonstration should take less than five minutes if everything is ready. The children then select their own colors and pieces for their work.

At other times, by using the same supplies, more specific requests may be given as to what should be made. The children could be asked to make a picture of some way to travel, a real or pretend person, or an animal. They can stretch their imagination and have very individual creations.

Crayons

Having boxes of new crayons is desirable, but be sure to save the pieces from old and broken crayons as there are beautiful effects that can be gotten only by using small pieces with their paper covering removed.

Flat crayon rubbings: Show the different effects that can be produced by rubbing a small, flat piece of crayon on the paper. Another color can be rubbed over the first one to observe the color change that happens. This is a more satisfactory way to color large areas than that of using the end of a crayon. Provide time to experiment with crayon scraps to create wavy lines, sudden dashes of color, or color combinations.

Rubbed impressions: Distinctive pictures can be created by placing a flat object or shape on the table, placing a paper over it, and rubbing a crayon across the paper. While holding the paper securely, by pressing one hand on the bottom edge, a short, flat crayon is rubbed in one direction only. Rub away from the hand that is holding the paper. Use leaves, paper shapes, string that is in a shape or design, or textured paper as a design under the paper. More than one color can be used. The paper can be moved to make more impressions of the same shape.

Crayon drawings: Any sincere attempt to draw a picture should be recognized. It is not desirable for a less talented child to try to copy the teacher's work or that of another child. Many times a few well placed lines are more creative and expressive than a meticulously colored picture. Allow a child to tell what he was thinking about when he made his drawing.

Individual designs: Individual designs are easily made by using rulers with crayons. Black lines are drawn across the paper by placing the ruler at different angles. The spaces are filled with different colors. Plaid patterns are made by placing the ruler horizontally and vertically for the lines. Draw some close together, and others far apart. Colors to fill the spaces change as they cross where the spaces intersect. Strips of stiff cardboard can be used in place of rulers. These designs can be used as covers for books or greeting cards.

Creating figures from shapes: Growing With Children Through Art, Aïda Cannarsa Snow, Reinhold Book Corporation, offers interesting ideas that can help individual creativity. The story, "The Circle That Shops For a Face," stimulates enthusiasm as the teacher demonstrates while she tells the story. The circle shops in different places to get his facial and body features. Individual creations made by the children produce fun with creativity. This idea is easily adapted to be used with other shapes or groups of shapes.

Ovals: Develop a story about several ovals who were tired of just being shapes with nothing to do. Draw a big oval, a middle-sized oval, small ovals, long thin ovals, and a small fat oval. The big oval calls the middle-sized oval to hop onto one end of him. Draw them being together. As each shape gets into his place, the shape of a rabbit develops. A bird is asked to drop two pink seeds that become eyes.

Geometric shapes (Draw the shapes as you tell the story): Once there were some shapes all scattered about. There were big and little round and square shapes. There were triangles. Some of them were tall and thin, some were short. There were large and small rectangles. Some rectangles were long and thin.

The shapes did not want to lie around being nothing but shapes. One round shape began to think the way a head does. He said, "Let's get together and have some fun."

All the shapes scrambled together to see what they could be. When they had their pictures taken, they looked like this (Figure 10-1). The children use pre-cut shapes to paste together.

Drawing From Life

Trees: In the fall, as the leaves are turning colors, take the children for a walk to observe the trees. Have them bring crayons, paper, and a cardboard support. When a tree is chosen as the one to be drawn, have them notice the size of the trunk as compared with its branches. Notice the bends and curves of the branches, and how much of them can be seen. Have them look carefully to see what colors there are, other than green and brown.

In the winter, and again in the spring, draw more pictures of the same tree.

Portraits: When children have had much experience observing pictures and objects, they become more aware of details.

After showing some pictures of portraits, have children take turns being models while a picture is studied. Have them look at the model's hair, and then look at the picture to see if the hair was painted only on the top of the head. Notice the way it covers the child's head. Using another model, place a hand on the top of his head and the other under his chin to show the space between. Ask the children where the eyes are. Help them to see that the eyes are halfway down. Look at the picture to see where the artist painted the eyes. Observe the other features in the same way.

Ask the children, "If an artist wanted to paint a picture of your head, what would he have to look at carefully?" A variety of answers will come. Encourage responses with, "You are thinking as an artist does." Then tell them they will be artists and draw a picture of the person sitting across from them. Many react as though a magic spell had been cast, and have fairly gasped, "An artist! I am an artist!" The dignity of feeling

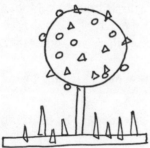

Figure 10-1

they are artists adds a comparable degree of effort and can result in surprisingly good portraits.

Drawing animals: This activity is a good one any time during the year. There should be a pet cage, or some suitable enclosure, for any pet that is to be in the room for a visit. It is advisable to know about any allergies children may have, as children have been known to get severe allergic reactions when an animal is in the room, even though they do not handle it.

After the children have had time to observe the animal and its actions, possibly holding it or feeling it, have them arranged in a circle with the animal in the center. Have them draw the animal as they see it. Some child may say, "I can't do it." When you ask, "Oh, when did you try it before?" he no doubt will say that he had never tried it. Then ask, "How do you know you can't do it if you have never tried?" Talk to him about the number of legs the animal has, the size of the head as compared with the body, etc. When he begins to draw any part of the animal, be sure to encourage him. You could say, "Were you joking with me? You said you could not do it, and you are doing it!"

Chalk

Some of the same work done with crayons can be done with colored chalk. The chalk, broken into small pieces, should be kept separated as to light, intermediate, and dark colors.

There are different ways to prepare the paper to prevent having dusty pictures.

1. Dip the paper into water and let the excess drip off.
2. Brush a thin solution of commercial liquid starch on a smooth, hard surfaced paper.
3. Wheat paste, in a solution of seven tablespoons of paste to one cup of water, can be brushed onto the paper.
4. Cover the paper with a sugar solution made of two parts of sugar to one part of water. Apply the chalk while the paper is wet. A spray of the sugar solution put over the finished picture will give it a shiny appearance.
5. A fixative spray can be applied when the picture is finished. Care should be taken when this is used, being sure there is good ventilation. The spray should not be directed toward other people as it can cause breathing difficulties.

MANY WAYS TO USE PAINTS

By the second week of school, paints can be introduced. Easels should be ready with a sufficient supply of paper available. There should be a can of water for cleaning brushes. Each color of paint should have its own brush.

Demonstrate the way a paint brush is pressed on the inside of the paint can to prevent drips and splatters. Show what happens when a brush full of paint is lifted without first pressing off the excess. Explain that the water is to be used when a brush is painted over a different color that is wet, causing them to mix on the brush. Dipping into the water everytime a brush is used dilutes the paint. Show the way colors are changed when they are mixed.

Mixing colors: To show what happens when colors are mixed, have six clear glass containers with water. Using food coloring, put yellow in three of them, red in two, and blue in one. Add one drop of blue coloring to one container of yellow. Let it drift around and observe the blending effects before you shake it. Add a drop of red to another container of yellow. Add a drop of blue to one of the containers having red. When colors are blended, the darker color must be added to the lighter color, a small amount at a time. Darker colors quickly overpower lighter colors, and must be added gradually. A second drop can be added if the shade is not satisfactory.

First paintings: Children should be permitted to experiment with the colors when they first use paints. What may appear to be a jumble of colors to an adult could be a satisfying experience for a child. Children must have freedom to explore the possibilities of the paints and to create. The symbol, or picture-making stage, will come after the exploring needs are satisfied.

When a child shows a completed picture, he should not necessarily be expected to name it. Colors and shapes may be his satisfaction. Showing the finished pictures offers ideas to others. To avoid unfavorable criticisms from the group, ask them to tell what they like about the pictures.

Watercolors: Tempera paint is available in solid cakes. These can be used as watercolor paints. They last quite a long time and are more satisfactory in the kindergarten than are the regular watercolors.

Finger Painting

Mixing: Finger paints can be prepared easily by using Vano starch and tempera powder paint. The powdered paint is stirred or shaken with the starch to a desired thickness. A suggested recipe is: half of a one-pound can of paint powder, one half cup of liquid starch, a small amount of liquid detergent. Shake together. The mixture should be thick enough to spread easily while not being runny. The detergent makes the cleaning easier.

Supplies: Paper used for finger painting should have a hard surface. Butcher paper is commonly used. Some grades of butcher paper absorb moisture quickly and "pill" when they are rubbed. While it is not desirable to use this type of paper for rubbing it with the hands, it can be used for blot printing. Paper with a waxed surface sheds the paint.

A table with a Formica top is desirable as it can be cleaned readily, and paint can be applied directly to the Formica to make blot prints. Pieces of Formica can be used at other tables that have been covered with newspaper.

The painting area should be located where there is easy access to a sink or pans of water for cleaning purposes.

Beginning to paint: When introducing finger paint, show the amount of paint that is to be used, as well as the different ways the hands and the fingers can work the paint. After spreading the paint with the flat part of the hand, use finger tips, the side of the hand, the heel of the hand, or a fist to rub lines and shapes. Give the children opportunities to explore the possibilities of the medium. After they have experienced the use of finger paints, other ways to use the paint can be shown and children can select their own way to paint.

Blot prints: Spread a coating of paint on Formica or a suitable paper. Create a picture by rubbing through the paint. If the paint is worked too long, it tends to dry. A little water on the hands, or more paint may be necessary. Lay a fresh piece of paper over the painted area, pat it down, and peel it off. Interesting effects are achieved by partially blending two colors to make a print. With too much paint, you cannot get a good print, as it tends to blur.

A different way to make a print is to spread paint evenly on one paper. Place another paper on the top. With a pencil or blunt object, draw something on the top paper, using a firm pressure. There will be a positive and negative picture when they are pulled apart. You must experiment first to determine the amount of paint to use.

Beautifully blended color designs can be achieved by first folding a paper in half. Open the paper and put dabs of different colors of paint on the fold. Refold the paper. Pressing firmly on the fold, rub away from it. Different pressures on different parts of the paper produce interesting effects when the paper is opened. Instead of putting the paint on the fold, paint could be quickly spread over the paper that has been folded. Refold it and press in different places before opening it.

Implement painting: The use of implements offers many picture and design possibilities. Have such things as spools, plastic forks, small blocks of wood that have grooves or a raised grain, small jar lids, cut bits of sponge, sponge cut into shapes, a section cut from the top of a Vano bottle to make wavy lines, a chunk of plastic clay with lines etched on it, or anything that could make interesting lines or shapes when it is twisted or rubbed across the paint. Some of the implements could be dipped into the paint and printed on the paper. Experiment first to be ready to briefly offer ideas as a spark for the children's creativity.

Panels: Cut panels of colored paper. Have two colors of paint that will contrast well with the color of the panels. Using a small amount of each color, blend them gently with the fingers to have both colors show. Lay the panel over the paint, and pat it gently. Interesting effects are achieved by putting a little black paint in a few spots on the original design. Or, a little black paint could be carefully dribbled onto the finished panel. If you have gold paint powder, just a pinch of it sprinkled on the wet paint gives it a dramatic appearance. When the panel is dry, glue folded strips of black paper at the top and bottom of the panel. A cord through the top fold has the panel ready for hanging.

CREATING WITH CLAY—PLASTICINE AND CERAMIC

Plasticine clay can be ready for use at any time. The only other supply that is needed is a clay board, or some other protection for the table. Using clay helps to develop hand muscle control, and should be encouraged. Children can develop skills, shaping and forming objects, that aid them when they use ceramic clay.

Ceramic clay: Ceramic clay should be introduced by a directed lesson. Aprons should be worn, the tables covered with paper, and small bowls of water provided for each two or three children. Have a piece of clay about the size of a small orange ready for each child.

Bowls: An easy project for the first use of ceramic clay is to make a bowl or thumb pot. If you are not experienced with the use of this clay, experiment to get the feel of the clay and the amount of water that may be needed on the finger tips to erase cracks. The clay dries when worked with for very long. Hold the ball of clay on the fingers of both hands. Press the thumbs into it while turning the ball, forming a bowl. The thickness of the bowl should be as even as possible. When cracks appear, the fingers must be dipped into the water. If large cracks are left, or the bowl has thin spots, it will break when it is fired. When the bowl has a satisfactory shape, opened paper fasteners can be used to scratch a design on the sides. Scratch the child's name on the bottom of the bowl, and set it aside to dry for several days. Drying takes from five to seven days, depending on the thickness of the bowls. If they are not thoroughly dry before firing, they are apt to shatter in the kiln.

Glazing: After the bowls have had their first firing, a clear or colored glaze is painted on for the glaze firing. Later projects may have color under-glazes used before a final clear glaze. When using the color glaze paints, the children must get as much color as possible on their brush, or the color will be lost in the firing. A clear glaze is painted directly over the under-glaze before the glaze firing. The glaze colors change when they are fired. Chips that are furnished with the paints let you see the final color.

SUMMARY

Children vary in their individual abilities in art expression. Their abilities in art may not relate to their expressions in other areas. Each child must be encouraged in all areas of learning. The child having difficulty expressing himself in art must have his efforts and contributions accepted and appreciated. All children should be encouraged to develop their ideas through individual styles and modes of expression.

The children who show a special aptitude for art expression should not be set apart for special praise, nor should their work be used as patterns for others to copy. The goal is to have each individual feel free to use the materials in a way that can best express his feelings. He is to feel that what he creates is his, and so it is right for him. It has been proven that children who are having learning difficulties in other areas can have their confidence increased by being able to express themselves artistically.

SEASONAL IDEAS

These activities may be individualized to suit the talents of each child. Allow the youngsters to select their own activities or a variation of the idea.

September

Trees: With a brush, paint a tree trunk and some suggestions of branches. Dip a small square of sponge into paint and gently pat it on for leaves. Small, flat pieces of crayons can also be used to make trees.

Apples: Cut corners from colored paper, or make them free-hand with crayons or paint.

Mural: Mount houses, trees, and people.

House book: Using a paper cutter, cut the shape of a roof from one side of sheets of construction paper. Staple three at one end to be a house book. Color the cover page as the front of the house. The pictures of things that belong in a house can be drawn or cut out and pasted in the book.

October

Pumpkins: Draw or paint Jack-O-Lanterns. Make pumpkins by the cutting-corners method previously described.

Black cats: Have black construction paper that is cut into two-inch squares and four and one half by six-inch rectangles. Fold the rectangle in half by bringing the *short* sides together. To have the children understand where they will cut the legs, stand the folded paper to show that the open edges are where the legs will be. Put the open edges together, and cut the legs by cutting out a rectangular piece about one inch in from each side, and cutting up a little more than an inch to have sturdy legs. Put paste on one corner of the square and paste it on one end of the body. Cut a tail and two ears from the scraps (Figure 10-2). This method can be used to make different animals.

Casper the Ghost: Have a piece of string about twenty inches long for each child. Drape the string over a finger, having equal parts of the string on each side. Lay this on a table. Push the string out to form arms. Children may help each other with the string. Place a piece of white paper over the string. Hold it firmly at the bottom edge. Children have better success when they stand to press on the paper. Using a piece of black crayon, rub over the paper in one direction to have Casper appear. Oval shapes for eyes and a mouth can be added (Figure 10-3).

Witches: Cut four black triangles for each child. When they are pasted, the paste is put only on the tips of the triangles. The triangle to be the hat is pasted on first, and positioned close to the top of the page. Then a face is drawn to join the hat. Imagination is used to draw funny features and scraggly hair. The next two triangles are pasted on to be the body. They may puff slightly. Arms are drawn with the hands holding a

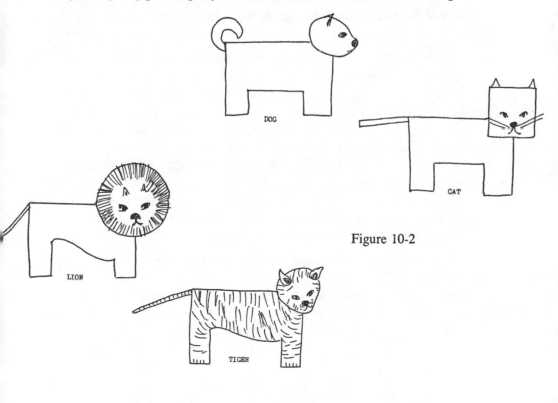

Figure 10-2

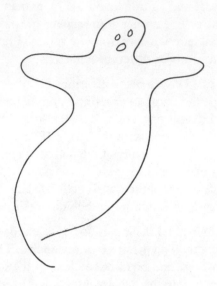

Figure 10-3

broom stick. The fourth triangle is the bottom of the broom. Add legs and feet (Figure 10-4). Other things could be drawn on the picture.

Owl: Materials needed: Six-inch paper bags, newspaper for stuffing, two-inch orange circles and one-inch black circles for eyes, black triangles for beaks, brown triangles for ears, brown crayons.

Prepare the bags by stapling the bottom of the folded bag on both sides to prevent the bottom of the bag from opening. Make a cut about three inches up in the middle of the open end.

Draw overlapping half circles on all sides of the bag to be feathers. Paste the black circles onto the orange circles and paste these eyes on the folded flap of the bag. Paste the beak just under the edge of the fold and attach the ears. Stuff the bag just enough to have it puff out. Tie or tape at the top of the cut. Spread the open two ends to be feet (Figure 10-5).

Fall leaves: Finger paint with two colors on the paper. Blend them to let the different colors show. Rich browns can be made by using a triad of colors, very carefully adding the darker colors to the lighter ones. When the papers are dry, leaf shapes can be drawn on the paper and cut out to be pinned on a mounted paper tree.

Figure 10-4

Figure 10-5

Rubbed leaves: Lay a piece of paper over a leaf and rub flat pieces of crayons over the paper. It will show the leaf shape and the veins of the leaf. The same leaf can be moved to be in different places, or a group of leaves can be arranged before rubbing the crayons.

Witches hats: Using twelve by eighteen inch construction paper, hold the short edges together and punch a cluster of about twelve holes near one corner. They should be an inch or so apart and not too close to the edge, getting some holes about five inches from the edge. The children decorate the paper with Halloween pictures. Have yarn cut into eighteen-inch lengths to be used for hair by putting the ends of a piece of yarn into two different holes and having it hang down. Shape the paper into a cone and staple it.

November

Indian: A life-sized Indian can be made by using a broom stick mounted to stand, newspaper, butcher paper, and paper bags. Have a child paint a face on a paper bag that is about eight inches wide. Stuff the bag with newspaper and drape a skein of black yarn for hair, taping it into position. Have children decorate a strip of butcher paper for a head band and make colored construction paper feathers to be stapled to the band. The completed head is then taped over the end of the stick. Gather the long sides of newspaper sheets to be taped, one at a time, to the stick. Start about halfway down the stick, overlapping the layers to the head. This is to furnish the body shape.

Tear off about five feet of butcher paper for a shawl, and a longer piece for the skirt. Have children first paint these papers brown, and then freely decorate them with Indian designs you have previously discussed. Each child paints his own idea of a design in his area. Wrap the skirt around the figure and tape it securely to the newspaper. The shawl is draped and taped to have it cross in front.

A papoose can be added by having a small bag painted to be a face. Stuff the bag and add yarn hair. Have the head extending from a larger bag that has been stuffed. Staple this to the ends of a strip of butcher paper to hang over the squaw.

Teepee: A large, standing teepee can be made by tearing off four strips of butcher paper about six feet long. Cut each strip on the

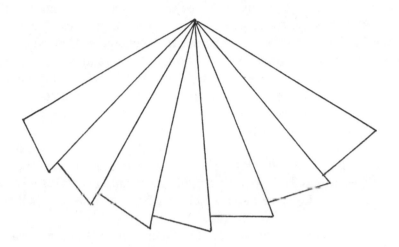

Figure 10-6

diagonal, as you would for a bias cut. Tape them together with brown paper tape. Every other piece must be reversed as is shown in Figure 10-6.

The bottom edge of the taped paper is trimmed to form a half circle. The teepee cover is painted brown and then decorated with Indian designs. Poles, about seven feet long, are lashed together and spread apart to be the frame. Staple the decorated cover to the top of the frame.

December

Hand prints: The method that is suggested here will make raised hand prints that appear to be real hands. The materials required are: plaster of Paris, tagboard strips that are two inches by twenty-four inches, drinking straws cut into about one and one half inch lengths, waxed paper, small papers for name tags, and Dap.

Dap is a plastic putty and is sold in hardware stores. One large can is needed for every twenty children. It can be reused a few times if it is kept wrapped in plastic between uses.

At a large working area, put out a square of waxed paper for each child to work with. Have a ball of Dap, about the size of an orange, on each paper. The Dap is to be flattened, and spread out as evenly and smoothly as possible, by using the palm of the hand. Do not use the fingers, as they are apt to leave impressions and grooves. The piece should be flattened to extend about one inch beyond the hand when it is in position to make a print. It should be about half an inch thick, and as smooth and even as possible. The teacher should supervise the placing of each hand, and pressing it into the Dap as far as possible.

When the print is made, press two pieces of straw into the Dap by the longest finger impression. They will provide holes for hanging the print. The child puts his name tag under the edge of the Dap to identify his piece. The teacher forms the strip of tagboard into a circle, or oval, and presses it into the Dap to fit around the print. This makes a collar to contain the plaster of Paris which can be poured at the teacher's convenience.

The plaster should be added *to* the water. Enough of the mix can be prepared to pour three or four prints at a time. It should be about the consistency of pancake batter. Immediately after pouring, hold the edges of the waxed paper and jerk it rapidly, back and forth, a few times to raise any air bubbles in the plaster mix.

When the plaster feels hard to the touch, scratch the child's name and the date on it. After an hour, if the mix was not too wet, the print will be set and the Dap can be peeled off to be used again. Remove the collars, and put the prints on pads of newspaper where they should continue to dry for at least one week. The straws may be removed then, or later, when the prints are painted. When all the prints are thoroughly dry, any rough edges can be sanded. The prints could be sprayed with gold enamel paint. By using gold paint powder, the children could paint their own prints.

Cards: Implements, finger painting, or prints could be used to make a cover. A printed verse could be pasted inside.

> Here is my hand,
> So tiny, so small,
> For you to hang
> Upon the wall.
> For you to watch
> As years go by,
> How we grow,
> My hand and I.

Wrapping paper: Cut sponges into shapes of trees or stars and glue them onto small pieces of wood. With not too much paint, and by gently patting sponges, make repeat designs on a suitable piece of paper.

Decorations: Using long, narrow, strips of colored paper, twist, loop, and staple them into free forms. Dot them with white glue and shake glitter on them.

January

Snowflakes: Use a heavy grade of tissue or a thin white paper, and cut into squares. Three folds are all that are necessary. Fold two corners together to make a triangle, then bring the two corners that are farthest apart together. Do the same thing one more time. Cut rather large, irregular pieces of paper from each of the three edges. Leave spaces between each cut. Furnish plenty of paper squares for experiments and mount some on a dark background.

Snowmen: Use the method of cutting corners from three sizes of squares. Children add decorations or arms and legs to show action, as they choose.

February

Hearts: Hearts can be cut freehand by holding a folded paper on its folded side, and then cutting a shape to look like an ice cream cone. Large and small hearts can be put together to make bees, dogs, butterflies, or people. Some of the hearts may be cut in half. Pipe cleaners can be shaped into hearts and glued to a paper, or shape stems on the hearts and stick them into a small amount of plaster of Paris, poured into a small paper cup, to make a bouquet.

String designs with paint: Fold a paper in half. Open the paper. Dip a piece of string into paint, keeping one end clean for holding. Starting at the top, let the string go down one side of the paper in twists and turns as it lands, having the end extend at the bottom. Fold the other side over. Lay a magazine on the top, and while holding it in place, pull the string out by making full sweeps from side to side, the width of the paper. A string with a different color could be used for a second pulling. The designs could be considered finished, or accents could be added and spaces colored with crayons if they suggest something special.

March

Creative pictures: On 9 x 12 inch sheets of white construction paper make wiggly lines by using a marking pen. The marks can be made quickly, and each should be quite different (Figure 10-7). When the group is gathered, show one of the papers. Suggest that the line could be a part of something. Turn it different ways and have the children tell what the line might be: an arm, a head, or another part of the body, a part of an animal, and so on. Ask for suggestions as to what could be added to make it become a picture of something. Use two or three samples by quickly adding lines and coloring spaces. Then spread the papers to offer a free choice, permitting the children to select one that may suggest an idea. Some of the pictures they develop may be designs, but most of them will have titles. This activity is worthy of another attempt at a later date. It is good for developing individual ideas.

April

Easter baskets: A sturdy basket that can have repeated uses requires a plastic container for each child. Margarine bowls are good to

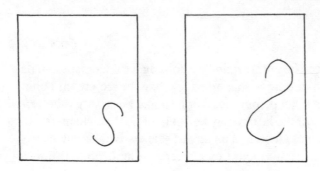

Figure 10-7

use for this project. Have newspaper cut into circles or rectangles, according to the shape of the bowls. Cut enough newspaper to provide each child with six pieces that will fit over a bowl. Mix a pan of wheat paste that will furnish about one half of a cup of paste for each child. Put some paste into each bowl. Cover the working areas with newspaper and have the children wear aprons. Demonstrate by making one bowl. Completely cover one piece of the cut newspaper with the paste, putting it on smoothly and not too thickly. Put another piece on the pasted one, and spread more paste. Continue until all six pieces are stacked evenly. The stack should be turned over and paste put on the dry side. Any extra paste in the cup is put back into the pan. The cup is then turned upside down and the pasted papers are draped and pressed around the cup to shape a basket. Name tags are patted onto the bottoms of the baskets. The next day the cups will slip out easily, and the baskets can dry on the inside. If too much paste was used, they will need an extra day to dry.

Have pictures of flowers from wallpaper or other sources for the children to select and cut out to decorate the baskets. After the flowers are cut, the baskets are painted by using a mixture of fingerpaint. While the paint is wet, the flowers are pressed into place. When the paint is dry, holes can be punched for pipe cleaner handles.

Easter eggs: Materials needed: small balloons, wheat paste, strips of newspaper and strips of paper towel, tempera paint.

Blow up and tie the balloons. Cover the balloon with wheat paste. Apply the strips of newspaper by beginning at the tied end and running them to the other end and back down to the tied end. They go on more smoothly this way than by trying to go around the balloon. When the balloon is covered, put on more paste and more strips. Put on several layers and let dry.

Put on more wheat paste and cover the balloon with a final coat of paper towel strips. Let it dry again. When it is thoroughly dry, the egg can be painted in any way the child can express himself. Have some suggested ideas for possible designs.

Caterpillars: Learning about the life cycle of the caterpillar can incorporate art with science. The caterpillar is made by using 1½ x 12 inch strips of brown construction paper and small pieces cut into 1 x 4 inch sizes. The small pieces are pasted into circles, and are then pasted, or glued, onto the long strip. They are placed closely together, with the openings of the circles showing on the sides.

Put black dots for eyes and two feelers on the first circle. Colored paper dots, saved from those made by a paper punch, can make the caterpillar gay. Put a few drops of glue on the tops of the circles and then dip them into the colored dots. Save the caterpillars.

Cocoons: Materials needed are small balloons, inflated and tied; stacks of heavy tissue paper or newspaper cut into pieces of a size that will not wrinkle when put around a curved object; and wheat paste.

Cover the balloon with paste. Put pieces of paper on the balloon to cover it. Add more paste between each layer until there are three or four layers, or more if tissue is used. The next day they can be painted brown. Save the cocoons.

Butterflies: Ditto a butterfly shape on construction paper. There should be a second line about one fourth of an inch in from the edge as the center will be cut out. When the butterflies are cut, brush them with liquid starch and lay them on a square of colored tissue that is larger than the butterfly. The excess tissue is trimmed off. Have bits of tissue in different colors to be cut and put on the wings by using starch. Bend the wings up from the body.

The three stages of the caterpillar's life are then put together by using a branch, and by taping the caterpillar to it, having him appear to be crawling. The cocoon is tied on to hang down, and the butterfly can be taped or pinned on.

May

Coloring flowers: Have as many felt-tipped pens as possible to be used at a central place. The children use them rather quickly to outline the flower shapes (Figure 10-8). The papers are then taken to working areas to be filled in with color. They may be cut out or completed to become a picture.

Popcorn flowers: Put a little dry tempera paint powder over popcorn in a bag and shake it. The colored popcorn can be dipped in white glue to stick to stems that were drawn, and become hyacinths. They can be glued in clusters to tree branches to look like blossoms.

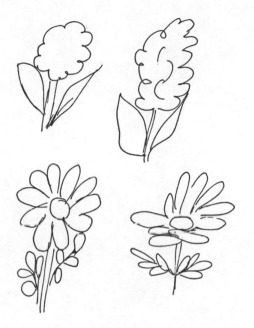

Figure 10-8

EXPERIMENTS
IN SCIENCE

11

Young children have a natural curiosity that should be nurtured. They want to explore the possibilities of the things they see. Within reasonable limits this should be encouraged and guided to help them solve their questions of "What is it?" and "Why is it behaving (or appearing) this way?" There must be firm limitations for safety: exploring electrical outlets or wiring, using any flame, and tasting unknown materials must be prohibited, and the reasons must be clearly understood.

For some children the kindergarten will be the first place where interesting and often exciting things happen to explain the immediate world around them. They will have a need for individual encouragement and guidance to explore on their own the possibilities of, or the reasons for, the things they see.

When you demonstrate an experiment, or suggest a problem to be solved, do not give all the answers. Let the children try to tell what they think might happen, and then to discover for themselves whether or not they were right. Do not be afraid to say you do not know an answer, but suggest ways the children might help to find an answer. Be sure to follow up with further clues the next day. Do not try to stop the solution. Have the materials out for individual experiments.

You should try out any experiments you plan to suggest for

children's use. You must be able to anticipate exactly what the outcomes will be.

USING EVERYDAY MATERIALS TO ESTABLISH
CURIOSITY—"WHAT," "WHY," AND "PROVE IT"

It is not necessary to have a big supply of science materials to conduct many interesting experiments. Materials that are in the yard, the room, or commonly used at home can furnish opportunities for learning. Science should include a series of problem-solving activities.

Have a special place or table to be the science space. You can put a sign by it labeled WHAT—WHY. Class collections or any unusual things brought in can be put there for observation. Magnifying glasses can be left there for close observation of items. Have the displays maintained in a proper order. This is good training for children to keep things sorted. Change the displays often enough to maintain interest. Have the materials that have been used for demonstrations arranged to permit individual uses.

After the class has been introduced to the science corner, allow individual children to work with various science materials of their own choice. Work with them, or have an aide do so. When a child is able to, have him demonstrate for the class or teach other children how they may do experiments. Schedule a free time when the children may work with the science materials by themselves or in groups.

Toys: There is more pleasure and lasting satisfaction to be had from creating usable toys than from the use of a pre-made toy that does not require any skill to operate, or that does not offer further creative possibilities. There is reasoning skill needed to build things to balance, to use wheels and axles efficiently, and to plan the parts to satisfy the needs of use or the shape desired. Use blocks, odd sizes and shapes of pieces of wood, snap-on wheels, old film reels and spools that can be used as wheels or pulleys. There are also good commercial toys that lend themselves to creative construction.

Field Trips

Before you go on any trip, have it planned and discussed with the group. The more extensive the trip, the more carefully the planning should be done. The children should understand the purpose of the visit—what they are to observe, and what they hope to learn. Pictures and stories related to the type of visit they are to have should be used in the days prior to the trip. For safety, there should be one adult for each four children taking the trip. The rules of courtesy for invited guests should be evident during the visit.

Each trip should have follow-up discussions and activities in the classroom. Stories can be composed, pictures drawn, or some cooking done if the visit was to a place producing or supplying a food product.

Short walk: Interesting collections can be gathered on a short walk if plans are made about what is to be found. Find as many different leaves as possible, to be pressed and mounted later; rocks of different colors or shapes can be collected; hunt for seeds from trees or weeds (these can be observed in the field or in the room to see the way they scatter naturally). When seeds and leaves are collected, they can be identified as to the tree or plant that bore them. Children learn that an apple leaf cannot come from a maple tree, or a blackberry vine with its leaves, from a fir tree. They learn that the seeds reproduce only their own kind.

Rocks: Interest in discovering the differences in rocks can be developed. Rocks can be selected according to colors, formation, or shapes. Those found by moving water often have been worn to become interesting shapes. By rubbing heavy sandpaper over a stone, or by rubbing two soft rocks together, sand can be created. Rocks can be broken to observe the way the inside differs from the weathered outside.

Light and Dark

Shadows: Using a flashlight or the light from a slide projector, have the children make hand shadows. What causes the shadow? Have them see their own shadows, in sunlight if possible, or by artificial light. Observe the shadows when the light comes from a low position, or overhead. How are they different? Why?

Temperature

Thermometer: As the temperatures of the days are noticed and mentioned, the use of a thermometer is included. A simple replica is made by making a long, stiff piece of cardboard to represent a tube with the degrees numbered. Cut slits at the top and bottom of the tube. Insert white and red ribbon sewn together in equal lengths and joined to form a loop. As the outdoor temperature changes, the ribbon can be moved to have the red part indicate the proper degree. A child can report whether that meant it was warmer or colder.

Aquarium

Frogs: One of the most interesting and informative projects you can have is to raise frogs. They take the least amount of care and afford two to three months of active observation of the life cycle of a frog. Use a large aquarium. It is much more satisfactory and more apt to be successful than trying to use a jar.

Using a large container will require buckets of pond water, with the eggs, to be brought to school, meaning that you, parents, or older students will be called upon to furnish them. They are worth the effort. The eggs and water should be taken with their natural growth to have food for the tadpoles when they hatch. Have the aquarium where the children can gather around it to observe the water life. They may see many water insects swimming around, and also plant life that is new to them. Using the magnifying glass while observing the specimens can be most fascinating.

The tadpole can be clearly seen jerking around in the egg when it is about to hatch. The tiny tadpole appears to be just a minute fish when it is swimming around. As they grow, they can be observed eating the plant leaves in the water.

To keep the water aerated, as is necessary for life, every few days scoop up a can of the water, hold up about twelve inches, and pour it back. Do this five or six times, and oxygen is replenished. If much water evaporates, add more pond water if possible, or collect rain water.

When the tadpole has his four legs he stops feeding from the plant growth and absorbs food from his tail as it shrinks. It is good to have a screen over the top of the aquarium when the frogs develop, or they may hop out. They should then be released, or taken home to be released to find their natural food.

Moss garden: Cover the bottom of an aquarium with sand. Place pieces of moss, with the soil in which they grew, on the sand. Moisten the soil and cover the top of the aquarium to retain the moisture.

The following are good for individual experiments.

Tin can telephone: Activities have been suggested in the chapter on training for auditory skills to feel and become acquainted with sound vibrations. This can be continued by making a "tin can telephone." Punch a hole in the bottom of two small cans. Put the ends of a long string through the bottoms of the cans and tie them to prevent their coming out. A waxed string will carry the sound better than a fuzzy one. Each fiber can carry off some of the vibrations. Two children using the phone should stand apart with the string taut and not resting on anything. One child holds the can to his ear while the other one talks into his can. To demonstrate the sound vibrations to two at a time, two children can hold the cans to their ears, with the string stretched, and someone can scratch or pluck the string.

Banjo: Stretch different lengths of rubber bands around an open box. Pluck the bands to hear the different pitches. Put something behind the longer bands to stretch them more, and then hear the tones. Do tightly stretched bands create higher or lower tones?

Sound travels in air: Hold an empty jar by the ear. Tiny sounds that are in the air will be heard. Fill the jar with water, place it on a table, and rest your ear over the jar. There will be no sound.

Sound travels through wood: Place a watch by an ear to hear the sound. Then place the end of a ruler to have it rest in the ear. Put the watch at the other end. The sound is louder.

Tap a pencil on a table. Place an ear on the table and then tap the pencil. What is the difference in the sound?

Sound travels through water: Tap some rocks and hear the sound. Then put the rocks in a jar of water. Put an ear by the jar and tap the rocks. What is the difference in the sound?

Electricity

Children are sometimes frightened by electric storms. The more they can understand electric storms, the better prepared they will be for them. They should be instructed in the ordinary precautions to avoid unnecessary dangers from lightning. They can learn how the storms happen, and that electric power can be helpful and is all around us in a small way. They can also learn that thunder is only the noise. When they hear thunder, the dangerous part has passed.

Static electricity: Comb a child's hair during cold weather. Hold the comb close to the hair after combing.

Shred some fine textured paper. Rub a blown balloon on your hair or on some wool. Bring it close to the paper.

Rub a plastic ruler or a comb the same way. Bring it close to the paper.

Rub a balloon on wool or fur and put it by a wall.

Tie two balloons to strings. Hold them by the strings and rub them with a piece of fur or flannel. Bring them close to different objects. Try putting your hand between them. Try to bring them together. What happens each time?

Experimenting with Household Supplies

Before you demonstrate the experiments for the children, try them to become familiar with the amounts of materials to use and their reactions. Try other combinations to discover what happens.

Coal garden: Use a large dish that is at least two inches deep because the growth that forms will spread.

Put a few small pieces of coal into the dish. Using one part of ammonia and six parts each of salt, bluing, and water, sprinkle the salt over the coal. Sprinkle the bluing and water over the coal. Add a few drops of food coloring. By the next day there should be an interesting display. When the action appears to slow, add a spoon each of salt and bluing. The dish should be on something that is covered, as the growth will go over the sides. Using drops of food coloring in different colors adds beauty.

Sight and taste: Have the children hold out their hands. Put a pinch of salt in one hand, and a pinch of sugar in the other. Put the same ingredient in each left or right hand. Ask them to tell by looking, which hand holds the salt. Then use the tips of their tongues to prove it. Before doing this stress the point that children are *never to taste a material they are not sure is safe.*

Smell: Have several small containers with different ingredients that have distinguishable odors: Peppermint, cinnamon, vinegar, crushed banana, peanut butter, mustard, orange, lemon (twisting the rind releases the fragrant oils), and soap. Have the children try to identify as many as they can. These can be left on the science table for individual attempts.

Taste and smell: Use a crisp apple and a sweet onion (be certain that the onion is not strong or bitter). Ask a child to volunteer to eat a tiny piece of one and then the other without seeing them, and while holding his nose tightly. Without the sense of smell, the sensation in the mouth will be the same if the textures are the same. Use a very small bit of each one. Let others try the experiment.

Liquids that do not mix: The terms "liquid" and "solid" are not too difficult for most children to understand when they are demonstrated and used frequently.

Color some water. In small containers demonstrate some liquids that mix with water: vinegar, syrup, milk, and the like. Then in a small bottle (a pill bottle can be used), pour some colored water and add mineral oil. Let them observe the reaction. Shake it and watch what happens.

Put clear Karo syrup with a few drops of color into a small bottle and mix them. Add mineral oil. Turn the jar over and observe the liquids. Shake it and watch what happens.

Leave the tightly sealed bottles of nonmixing liquids on the science table for observation and handling. They might be by signs that say, "Shake Me."

Density of liquids: While the term "density" is not expected to be learned, children can learn that some liquids are thicker than others. In one small jar put water and a marble. In another put clear syrup and a marble. Have the jars on the science table by "Turn Me" signs to observe the differences in the action.

Changes Created in Foodstuffs During Preparation

Some ingredients change by being mixed with others (they may dissolve or become thickened; heat or agitation may change them). When planning a project using foodstuffs, show the individual ingredients in their natural state. Taste the uncooked fruits or vegetables.

Seasonings may be identified by odor. Then show the way they are to be prepared to change their texture or appearance. Let the children share in the preparation after identifying the ingredients.

Making butter: This is especially apropos after a trip to a dairy, or during a farm unit. Have the children tell about the ways they enjoy cream and whipped cream. Using a rotary beater, children can whip the cream. They tire easily and may not be able to continue the necessary whipping. You may have to finish while they watch, or use an electric mixer. Salt may be added, or the sweet butter can be spread on crackers to enjoy.

Making soup: After a trip to a grocery store or a vegetable farm, the children cut up vegetables to be cooked. Have the children taste the raw vegetables. You may want to use a soup bone. Show it and explain what it is and why it is used. Since it takes long simmering, it can be served the next day. Let them decide whether or not they can taste carrots, parsley, celery, potatoes, onions, etc., or whether the flavors blend.

Pumpkin: If you have a pumpkin for a Halloween Jack-O-Lantern, a face can be painted on it instead of cutting it. After Halloween it can be washed, cut into pieces with the shell cut off, and cooked in a small amount of water. Mash it and add brown sugar to sweeten it. The children can decide how they feel about its taste. Save the seeds for planting.

Bread: Many children have never seen yeast cause bread dough to rise. Whether you want to make bread or not, it is informative for the children to see what happens when a yeast solution is mixed with flour and is left to rise.

Temperature changes: Children can see sugar dissolve in water. They can also observe the changes in the mixture when heat is applied. A recipe for lollipops is:

2 cups sugar
⅔ cup light corn syrup
1 cup water
food coloring
flavoring (1 tsp. mint, orange, or lemon)

Combine all ingredients except the flavoring. Place over heat and stir until dissolved. Use a candy thermometer and let boil to 280°.

Turn the heat off and keep the pan on the burner until the thermometer registers 300°. Remove the pan from the burner. Add the flavoring. Spoon a tablespoonful of the candy syrup over toothpicks that have been arranged on foil wrap. They harden quickly and take about thirty minutes to prepare after cooking begins. Children can measure the ingredients. Cooking boiling sugar is too dangerous for them to handle, but they can observe the thermometer changes. One recipe makes about sixty thin lollipops that are about two inches in diameter.

Applesauce: This is one of the easiest cooking projects. Children bring apples—one large one for a child. Show them the sugar and cinnamon that will be added. Each child washes and cuts his own apple. Apple corers and cutters are quick and easy to use. The child centers the cutter over the stem end, presses it down, and the unpeeled sections are put into the kettle that has a small amount of water in it. Cut pieces can be starting to cook as other children come to cut their apples and add them to the pot. Just the cores are thrown out. Any bad spots can be cut off with a small paring knife while the apple wedge rests on the table. The main group is busy (preferably with the teacher or an aide) at another activity while a small group is preparing their apples. The sauce will be cooked within an hour, but will not be ready to serve on the same day. The cooked sauce must be pressed through a collander to remove skins and any bits of core. Add the sugar and cinnamon after the sauce is strained.

An aide may supervise the cooking and preparations while the main group is otherwise occupied.

The red house with a star inside: For a story on the day that the applesauce is cooked, children enjoy hearing about a child who wanted something special to do. His mother told him to see if he could find a round red house that has no doors or windows, but it has a star inside. The boy thought that sounded like fun, but he did not know where to look. He went out and met a friend. He asked his friend, but the friend did not know where it could be. He talked to his dog about it, but his dog just wagged his tail. Then he saw grandfather sitting in the shade under the big apple tree. Johnny went over by his grandfather to tell him about his problem. Grandfather smiled and told him that he might need the help of a wind fairy. Johnny did not know how that would help. Just then the little breeze that was blowing became stronger and shook the tree's branches. A round red apple dropped to the ground. Johnny picked it up and looked at it a bit. "This is round and red. It has no doors or windows. Could it have a star inside?" Grandfather said, "Let's find out." He cut the apple across the middle instead of starting by the top, and there was the star!

The story situation has merely been sketched. You can add the conversations and descriptive actions. As you tell what the grandfather did, cut an apple the same way to show the star. Have a few other apples to cut in the same way, and then to cut into small pieces for the children to eat.

DEVELOPING SCIENCE CONCEPTS
USING "NATURE'S HOUSES"

When children are becoming acquainted in the fall, and telling about their families and homes, there is probably some discussion about the different materials that are used to make houses. This is a good time to introduce the study of the way living things are housed in nature. Any shelter for a living and growing thing is its form of a house as humans term it. This affords an opportunity for some children to contribute valuable offerings for the science table, and the individual recognition that they may need can often be found by their bringing shells and other materials. Insecure children can develop a feeling of importance by contributing even minor offerings that are recognized.

Shelled animals: Many living organisms carry their shelters with them. Collect samples of shelled animals: oysters, clams, snails, hermit crabs, muscles, barnacles. You may also have a "visiting" turtle.

Nesting animals: When you display used birds' nests explain that the nest is no longer in use and does not deprive a bird of his home. Try to have different types of nests, if possible, to show the intricate and skillful ways they were constructed.

Bees' nest: Many people are allergic to the sting of a yellow jacket and have exterminators fumigate a hanging nest. If you can be fortunate enough to obtain a nest that is no longer used, peel off some of the outside covering to show the layers in it and the individual cells.

EASY WAYS TO LEARN ABOUT:

Air, Its Forces and Uses

When you notice the clouds or the trees being moved by wind, ask what is happening. Why are the clouds (or the trees) moving? What is wind? Permit them to discuss it. Guide them to understand that it is the air that is moving. Can you feel air? Feel with your hands. Now hold your hands out and sweep them back and forth. Can you feel the air? Do you need air? Why? The following experiments are more valuable when done individually.

Air Has Force

Holding paper: To help the children understand that air is a substance that can exert pressure, have two square pieces of paper that are the same size. Lay one on your opened hand. Ask what it will do when you turn your hand on its side. If they say it will fall, turn your hand and show that they are right. Then tell them to watch as you turn your hand, but you turn in a circle while the paper remains pressed against your hand. Why did the paper stay on your hand? What held it there? Let them try it.

Show the two pieces of paper again to show that they are the same. Hold one in a horizontal position and let it float down. Let the children describe the way it moved. Why did it not fall straight down? Do it again to be certain that all children observe what is happening. Help them grasp the idea that it was sliding on the air. Then crumple the other piece of paper into a ball. Ask what will happen when you hold it up and let it drop. Do it; why did it drop as it did? Have pieces of paper for them to use to observe the actions as they experiment. Hold a flat piece and a crumpled piece at the same height. Which one will reach the floor first? Why? Is one heavier than the other?

Parachute: To further extend the idea of the support that air can give, make a parachute. Use a cork or a Styrofoam ball to be the dragging force. Toss it up to show the air pressure under the fine cloth.

Air takes up space with force: Have an aquarium or a large clear container with water in it. Show an empty glass. Ask if there is anything in the glass. Have children feel in the glass to tell how it feels. Push the glass, open end down, into the water. While it is under the water ask how the inside of the glass should feel now. Explain that you must wipe the water from your hand and the outside of the glass, but that you will not touch the inside of the glass. How do you think it will feel? Have them feel it. Then crumple a piece of paper and put it in the glass. Push it straight down again. Pull it up and wipe the outside. Why is the paper dry? Some children immediately say, "You are magic!" Let them try it and try to discover the answer.

When it has been recognized that air filled the glass and held the water out, prove it. Push the glass under and then gradually tip it on its side to observe the air bubbles.

Push the glass straight down and suddenly release it. Why did it jump up?

Put the glass into the water and let it fill with water. Pull the glass partly out of the water and observe what the water in the glass does. Why is the water staying in the glass?

Pick up a paper: Use a straw and a small piece of paper or a paper cup with a hole in the bottom. Center it on the paper and suck the air from the straw or the hole in the cup. The air pressure inside becomes weak and permits the paper to be lifted.

Floating rock: Use a small rock from the yard, a piece of pumice, and a jar of water. Hold the rock over the water and ask what will happen when you drop it. Do it. Then hold the larger piece of pumice rock the same way, ask what will happen, and do it. Why did it float? Have them examine the pumice to solve the problem.

Air Has Weight

Weighing air: Balance a thin stick by pushing a long pin through a cardboard box to have the pin extend up about two inches. Press the stick to the end of the pin at its midpoint. Another way to balance the stick is to tie it and hang it.

Blow one balloon with a small amount of air and tie it off. Blow one more to be much larger. Hang them from the ends of the stick to see what happens.

Warm Air Takes More Space than Cold Air

Stretch (expand) air: Blow up two balloons to the same size. Tie one where it will feel heat. Tie the other one by a cold window. Check their sizes the next day.

Fire Must Have Air

Using flame must be done only by the teacher. Children can learn an important safety precaution when they understand that cutting off the source of air will put out a fire. They should be instructed in the proper procedures to extinguish any fire that may get to their clothing. It is more impressive when they see a flame die when the air is cut off. Children must be firmly impressed with the dangers of playing with matches.

Extinguishing a candle: Stand a candle in a jar and light it. Put a lid on the jar and see how quickly the flame uses all the air that was in the jar. Impress it on the children's minds that they must roll on the floor or the ground immediately if their clothes catch on fire. Running will add more air for the flames.

How Seeds Develop

To better understand the way plants are able to absorb what they need for growth, the fine root hairs should be observed. Seedlings should be started to grow in a way to have the roots visible.

Sprouting large seeds: Line a glass with a piece of a blotter having it press against the inner side. Show the dry blotter in the glass. Pour in about an inch of water. Watch what happens to the blotter. Add more water if necessary. Place seeds, such as beans or corn, between the blotter and the glass, about half way down the sides. Daily gardeners can assume the responsibility of checking to see that there is water in the bottom of the glass. Place them on a window sill to be observed each day. Watch for the first signs of growth. Date the "planting" time and record which seeds begin to grow first. Observe what happens to the seed as the roots and stems emerge. Use magnifying glasses to better see the fine root hairs that develop.

When the true leaves begin to develop (the first two leaves are sources of energy and do not have the shape of the plant's true leaves), carefully remove the blotter from the glass and gently peel away the root hairs. Have moistened potting soil ready and plant the seedlings.

Sprouting small seeds: Radish seeds develop quickly and easily by using sheets of paper towels. Wet the long side of the towel where the seeds will be placed. Arrange the seeds in a row, about two inches from the edge, and an inch apart. Lay another sheet on top, and repeat the process of placing seeds. When you have the seeds placed, roll the towels into a fairly snug roll and put a rubber band around it. Place the roll into a jar that has about two inches of water in it. The seeds should be at the top of the jar. The water level must be checked each day to prevent the paper towel from drying. Check the time it takes for the leaves to appear. Unroll the paper towels, observe the mass of hair roots. Have other radish seeds in soil.

Absorbing water: To prove that the roots absorb water, place a seedling in a small glass or tube of clear water. Put another into water that has red food color added. Observe the difference in the leaves. This is fun to do with cut flowers that show absorption easily, such as daffodils. Place the cut flowers in glasses of water that have food color. Observe the way the streaks of color extend into the flower petals. A piece of celery stalk will react in the same way.

Growing plants need water, air, and light: Have the children see what happens to plants that are deprived of water, air, or light. Let the soil for one plant dry until the leaves begin to droop. Will water help it? Cover one leaf on a plant with foil. After a few days, remove the foil. Is there a change in the leaf?

Place a plant to have it just to the side of a window, but away from the direct light. How does it affect the plant stems and leaves? After a few days, turn the plant halfway around. What will happen to the plant?

Where are the seeds: Have samples of foods that people enjoy by eating the seeds: peas and beans in their pods, an ear of corn, a sunflower, and nuts. Have the children identify the seeds.

What Magnets Can Do

Collect as many magnets as you can—large and small, horseshoe, bar, and round magnets. Some sets to be purchased include several magnets of different sizes and shapes and include metal rods and shaped pieces as well as iron filings. They are listed in the catalogs from supply houses.

When you have the magnets out for use, they should be checked each day to be certain some have not dropped and are clinging to a piece of metal on furniture. They should also be stored properly to retain their magnetism.

Attracting and repelling: When they are introduced, distribute two magnets to each child interested in using them. When he has completed his work, tell him to pass them to another child who has not yet had a chance to use them. Let them try to bring two magnets together and then turn one and try to bring the ends together. What happens? Some bar magnets have the north and south poles marked by "N" and "S." Have the children decide which ends attract each other and which ends repel.

Using other materials: Put out a variety of materials to discover which ones are attracted by a magnet. Guide the experiments to decide what is attracted. Provide a sufficient opportunity for the children to experiment with the reactions the magnets have when they are used with each other and with other materials. Use some sand or soil to decide whether it has some particles of iron in it.

Magnetic force passing through materials: Have the children place a magnet on a piece of paper, cardboard, plastic, cloth, glass, etc. to see whether or not another magnet on the other side will cling to it or be able to move the top magnet.

Iron filings will be less apt to be lost if some are sprinkled on a piece of tagboard and have a magnet moved about under it, causing the filings to move. Put one end of a bar magnet under the filings. Watch what they do. Then put the opposite end to the tagboard to see what the filings do. The filings can be poured back into the container for later use.

Jumping magnets: Put round magnets in a stack. Put a bar magnet that is the length of the height of the stack into the hole in the center. If it stays there, take it out and put it in with the other end up. It will jump out and land on the round magnets.

Hold a round magnet slightly above another one. When they are the right distance apart, the bottom one will jump to the other one.

Have the children think of as many uses for water that they can, both indoors and outdoors. List them. What would happen if plants did not have water, or if people did not have water?

Solid vs. liquid: When is water a solid instead of being liquid? How can you tell by looking at the thermometer that you might find ice out of doors? What are hail (raindrops passing through a freezing layer of air) and snow (water vapor in the clouds that get below a freezing temperature)? What happens when hail or snow gets warm?

Soap bubbles: A fun time can be had by blowing bubbles. For the bubble blowers, you can use wooden thread spools or a drinking straw. With the straw, cut two slits about one quarter of an inch deep across one end. Press the four tabs out. Dip them into the soapy water and blow gently. A little glycerin in the soapy water adds strength to the bubbles.

Water is absorbed: Children can see the way a sponge swells when it absorbs water. Then they can be shown two interesting experiments and decide why they happened as they did.

Break five toothpicks in half, being careful that the two parts do not separate. Place the bent back toothpicks on a dry dish, having their broken ends coming together in the center. Dip your finger into water and drip the water over the center of the picks. Watch the star form.

Cause a bear to come from hibernation. Draw a bear that is about

five inches tall. Cut enough of them from newspaper to provide each child with a bear. Tell the children that little bear went to sleep for the winter (as you fold his head, arms, and legs into the center, making almost a circle). Now it is springtime and little bear awakens. Place the bear on water in a pan and watch him unfold.

BOOKS TO USE WITH THE CHILDREN

Schwartz, Elizabeth and Charles. *When Water Animals Are Babies.* Holiday House, Inc. New York, 1970.

Carrick, Donald. *The Tree*. The Macmillan Company. New York, 1971.

Childcraft—The How and Why Library—Volume 8. *How Things Work*. Field Enterprises Educational Corporation. Chicago, 1966.

Craig, Gerald S., Etheleen Daniel. *Science Around You*. Ginn and Company, 1961. (Good for getting many ideas about water, plants, energy, simple machines, etc.)

McMillan, Polly Miller. *Little Lamb's Curls*. Lothrop Publishing Company, 1962. (A delightful story about the source of wool.)

Selsom, Millicent. "You and the World Around You." Doubleday and Company, Inc. Garden City, New York, 1963.

Shapp, Martha and Charles. *Let's Find Out About Air*. Franklin Watts, Inc. New York, 1963. (This offers simple experiments.)

Wyler, Rose. *The Golden Picture Book of Science*. Golden Press. New York, 1957.

Reference Books for the Teacher

Childcraft—The How and Why Library—Volume 3. Field Enterprises Educational Corporation. Chicago, 1965. (Ideas for the teacher concerning weather, the earth, and nature.)

UNESCO. "700 Science Experiments for Everyone." Doubleday and Company, Inc. Garden City, New York, 1958. (Experiments that are for both younger and older students.)

INDEX